NEW MEXICO POETRY RENAISSANCE

NEW MEXICO POETRY RENAISSANCE

EDITED BY
SHARON NIEDERMAN
AND MIRIAM SAGAN

FOREWORD BY ROBERT CREELEY

R·E·D
CRANE
BOOKS

SANTA FE

First Edition

Book design by MINDART STUDIO

Cover painting, *Santa Fe Fiesta*, 1921, is by William Penhallow Henderson

Manufactured in the United States of America

Library of Congress Cataloging-in-Publication Data

New Mexico poetry renaissance / edited by Sharon Niederman
and Miriam Sagan.
        p.   cm.
     ISBN 1-878610-41-4
     1. American poetry—New Mexico. 2. American poetry—20th century.
3. New Mexico—Poetry. I. Niederman, Sharon. II. Sagan, Miriam.
     PS571.N6N48 1994
     811'.540809789—dc20
                                        94-12905
                                         CIP

Red Crane Books
2008 Rosina, Suite B
Santa Fe, New Mexico 87505

CONTENTS

FOREWORD

First coming to New Mexico from New England in the early 1950s, I had no sense of how vast and transforming this human place would prove to be. Scale is immensely increased here, time moves in a measure of centuries, and people are only a small if particularizing instance of so-called life. It is as if we had here to leave our usual human situation and enter upon another imagination of what our lives are all about as well as how and where we live them. As simple a thing as a glass of water is different in New Mexico—just that water can be scarce indeed. To see some 200 miles without impedance is almost startling. Entering a small cave where others had once been over twenty thousand years ago changes all argument forever.

So D. H. Lawrence found this place wondrous, and Cabeza de Vaca long before him cried to witness its enduring peoples adapting of painful necessity to the newcomers. Echoes of all these voices are here, the entrepreneur's, the old survivor's. The mountains, the fragile, surviving rivers, the vastness of sky, distance of mesa, sun, sudden wash of rain, cold and heat—these too echo. Just as one will see traces of the sea that once covered much of this ground, language here carries its own history and habit, speaking its persons with vivid and local authority. Our own fossils and shells are in our words.

Yet the generalities quickly blur. Poetry is, if anything, literally specific to place and person alike. Perhaps the very fact of New Mexico's amplitude means one has to find a way to anchor, or else disappear. In Sandoval County in my own time there was something like an average of one person per ten square miles, and always more cows than people. If one thought to go somewhere, or to get back, it was always a long way. Therefore knowing the particulars of one's place was a necessity in every sense. It's a necessity as well for these poets.

Many have come to New Mexico looking for change, wanting something to bring them back to themselves or else give them new location. That's how I first got there, following friends who'd come before. It has always been a great human gathering point and a pass-through for those going west, or north, or back again, each with the determining habits of their company, the picture of the world they were born into. There were two old men I used to know in Taos, one of whom had been a ship's cook and made barley soup that could keep me going for days. These friends would go out on an isolated mesa at night and lie on their backs to look at the stars. One time they invited me to come with them, but I was too stupid to accept. I was into protest, like trying to burn down a billboard on the edge of town though it never worked. Things take more time in New Mexico.

So if you are at the beginning and the end at one and the same instant, where would you think that was? You can be at Puye, say, one minute, and then at Los Alamos, or move down the way to Gran Valle, or just head for Albuquerque, all thousands of years apart albeit close enough to get to nonetheless. Probably it's just that usual kinds of human location don't ever quite work here. But the place has paradoxically little to do with regionalism. People looking only for folklore need not apply.

Living here, I used to know just how far it was to the proverbial next town. For example, 350 miles to El Paso, 500 miles to Denver, 900 to Los Angeles, 1,200 to San Francisco, 1,000 to St. Louis, 2,000 to New York…I could even tell you the best way to go. Where did I think I was going? Certainly this present company would have helped as many, in fact, did then.

Now all the various definitions of poetry seem to shift and to contest, but the materials seem insistent—and the implicit act of making something out of words. These artifacts are constructs of language, one says, vulnerable to syntax and meaning. *So we will change the meaning, we will make new ways to go!* There will never be a poem or poetry without such heart implicit, or such things to say. Here you will find that integrity, and that art.

—Robert Creeley

INTRODUCTION

New Mexico the Muse

New Mexico serves as muse to the forty-one poets presented here. Whether they are natives, immigrants, or expatriates, they share this landscape as an inevitable source of nourishment which they celebrate.

The myth of New Mexico is as powerful as the desert itself under a blazing sky. First, there was the Santa Fe Trail, a route west to a place as distant and strange as the moon. Over this harsh, rutted road came the soldiers to tame this place; the traders to claim it; the railroads to drain it; the missionaries to train it; the anthropologists to name it; and finally, the artists and writers to explain it.

Colonists all, they shared a desire for a home away from home, a civilized outpost stimulating in its difference yet comforting in whatever familiarity they could reconstruct. The raw materials were abundant, and they made the most of them—coal and culture, wealth for the taking.

Those who came first were giants. Their work and events in their lives seem as familiar as the stories of distant relatives remembered from childhood. Streets and schools and parks are named after them. Gaspar Perez de Villagra, in 1609 Spain, wrote his epic poem *Historia de la Nueva México*, about his experiences in New Mexico. And Miguel de Quintana's poetry and prose were preserved as evidence in an investigation conducted by the church in the 1730s revolving around heresy. These documents remain from eighteenth-century Hispanic New Mexico. Some of them generated gossip that remains lively many years later. The freedom to create sought by them still exerts its magnetic attraction.

A look at New Mexico's literary history reveals a stunning observation: very little has changed over the years. The forces at work on writers and the themes they articulate generally remain constant in contemporary literature. Our current situation mirrors our history and the epic of encounter. These days, however, there is one significant development—now we hear from those who are "encountered" as well as those doing the "encountering."

Writers, then and now, continue to fall in love with New Mexico's land and light and to celebrate those magical elements. The collision of cultures is another unlimited, constant rich source of inspiration. Here, writers continue to be moved by the past, the homemade, and the handmade.

It is intriguing to learn how, early in the century, writers began drawing distinctions between insiders and outsiders, newcomers and old-timers—distinctions that continue to be made. And through it all, or perhaps because of it all, New Mexico has been a muse for the creation of prolific, beautiful, and controversial work.

In 1916, Chicago poet and editor Alice Corbin Henderson, the great-grandmother of the New Mexico literary scene, came to Santa Fe as a patient at Sunmount Sanitorium. As the editor of *Poetry* magazine, she was familiar with the best writing of her day and was acquainted with some of the most prominent poets of her time—such as Carl Sandburg, Ezra Pound, Vachel Lindsay, and Witter Bynner. That same year, Willa Cather arrived in New Mexico, as did Mabel Dodge Luhan, who soon departed Santa Fe for Taos to become a well-known patron of artists and writers.

The following year, 1917, Corbin Henderson produced a special issue of *Poetry* highlighting Native American chants and including the work of Harriet Monroe and Carl Sandburg. Then, in 1918, Mary Austin made her presence felt when she established the Santa Fe Community Theatre, providing writers with opportunities to create for the stage. Austin, Corbin Henderson, and Dodge Luhan continued to invite their influential, famous, and talented friends to New Mexico over the years.

By 1925, Corbin Henderson, Bynner, Haniel Long, Spud Johnson, and Lynn Riggs (a Native American who would write the play *Green Grow the Lilacs* on which *Oklahoma!* is based) were meeting weekly and calling themselves "The Rabble," shortened from the original "Rabelais Club." The developing Santa Fe scene produced a book with national impact, Corbin Henderson's collection *The Turquoise Trail: An Anthology of New Mexico Poetry*, published by Houghton Mifflin in 1926. Meanwhile, Spud Johnson moved to Taos in 1927, taking his *Laughing Horse* literary magazine with him. Along with *Laughing Horse* and *El Palacio*, the Santa Fe *New Mexican* published poetry about New Mexico written by those who now considered themselves "New Mexicans." The earliest incarnation of *New Mexico* Magazine, the *New Mexico Highway Journal*, appeared in 1923 and published verse.

The Great Depression did nothing to stifle New Mexico's literary output. Beginning in 1930 and lasting through the decade, the Sunday afternoon

Poets' Round-Ups, held in various Santa Fe gardens, were important gatherings. With the arrival of Walter L. Goodwin and his Rydal Press from Pennsylvania in 1933 publication of the Writers Editions Series began, including volumes by Alice Corbin Henderson, Peggy Pond Church, and Haniel Long. Also in 1933 the first New Mexico Roundtable on Southwest Literature was held in Las Vegas, headlined by John Crowe Ransom. Robert Frost read in Santa Fe in 1935, the same year Ina Sizer Cassidy was named state director of the New Mexico Federal Writers Project. In addition, Alfred Knopf and editors from Macmillan visited their New Mexico authors; and Henry and Clare Booth Luce also traveled here.

In the 1940s, repercussions of World War II were felt in New Mexico, especially because of the Manhattan Project in Los Alamos and a Japanese internment camp in Santa Fe. As a result of these events, the mood became somber, though Oliver LaFarge and May Sarton wrote in Santa Fe while Conrad Richter and Erna Fergusson were based in Albuquerque.

In the 1950s and 1960s, other writers came to New Mexico—John Nichols, Stanley Crawford, Mark Medoff—and by the early 1970s, Rudolfo Anaya described the New Mexico Hispanic experience in *Bless Me Ultima*. Writing in poetry, prose, and traditional storytelling forms, N. Scott Momaday and Leslie Marmon Silko focused on the Native American experience, while Frank Waters and Tony Hillerman popularized the Indian experience. Keith Wilson at New Mexico State University in Las Cruces and Gene Frumkin at the University of New Mexico in Albuquerque became influential as poets and as teachers. Margaret Randall, with her publications from abroad, kept links to Latin America alive. And Robert Creeley brought with him the winds of change from the Beats and Black Mountain College.

Today, New Mexico serves as muse for several generations of working poets. The sheer number of living poets concentrated together here, listening to each others' voices and borrowing each others' influences, has created a critical mass that can only be called a renaissance. Like the San Francisco poetry renaissance of the 1960s, which it resembles in that public performance and a community-based audience are key factors, the New Mexico poetry renaissance is composed of disparate voices partially rooted in the Spanish traditions of poetry and letters and the Indian oral tradition.

Beat writers such as Jack Kerouac and Allen Ginsberg influenced the poets of New Mexico, who exult in writing about personal experience and the search for an ecstatic vision, while breaking the bounds of formal structure. And Gary Snyder's emphasis on an ecologically-based view of nature can be seen here, as well as Ginsberg's exuberant poetics and lines based on the human breath. Charles Olson, the granddaddy of American contemporary poetics, emphasized that American poetry should sound like American speech. This idea influenced the work of New Mexican poets, particularly the storytelling strain in the poetry of Simon Ortiz and Leo Romero. When Robert Creeley settled in Placitas in the 1960s, he also brought an emphasis on ordinary speech with him from Black Mountain College. As a teacher and eminent presence, his work reinforced the Beat influence.

In this collection of living poets, those from the 1960s can be considered the first generation. During this time Larry Goodell, Simon Ortiz, Gene Frumkin, and Keith Wilson emerged as poets. And the Institute of American Indian Arts in Santa Fe brought Native American poets into contact with their gifts. An important anthology, *The Whispering Wind: Poems by Young American Indians*, brought many New Mexico poets into print for the first time in 1972.

The second generation of poets, including Joy Harjo, Harold Littlebird, Jimmy Santiago Baca, Arthur Sze, Jim Sagel, Mei-mei Berssenbrugge, and Leo Romero, tended to be academically trained. In 1976, the Rio Grande Writers Association published an anthology, *Voices from the Rio Grande*, based on a convergence that began to give shape to the growing movement of contemporary writers.

Newer writers to emerge as strong voices include poets Joan Logghe, Judyth Hill, and Mary McGinnis. They are part of a third generation of influence, for if Leo Romero was influenced by Simon Ortiz, then Mary McGinnis would cite Romero's work as a source of inspiration.

Other poets continued to work quietly off the beaten track before publishing books and chapbooks. Rebecca Seiferle raised children and goats outside Farmington; Renée Gregorio brought what she had learned in England to Taos. As these newer poets write and publish, there are no doubt even younger poets, beyond the scope of this anthology, waiting to add their voices to the stream of New Mexico poetry.

The living poets of New Mexico are, as a rule, romantics rather than classicists. Their poetry is often based on a love, even a glorification, of the natural world. Since nineteenth-century England, this kind of romanticism has been a response to industrialization and the destruction of the environment—what William Blake called the "dark satanic mills." As New Mexico remains a haven, if a threatened one, in a world bent on mining, controlling, and profiting from nature, the stance of New Mexico poets is often one that seems to say, "We are still in Eden, if an endangered Eden."

The romanticism of New Mexico's poets is an American romanticism— it is a love not only of land but of family, not only of adventure but of traditional roots. The act of writing becomes a ceremony for those seeking to affirm tradition. Yet these poets cannot be called isolated or even regional, since their work consolidates time and space. John Brandi is equally at home in the Himalayas and in Corrales; Arthur Sze might suddenly find himself, through his writing, in China; and Joan Logghe's Española is both nearby and exotic.

Federico García Lorca and Pablo Neruda are powerful influences on New Mexico poets. Frida Kahlo functions as a muse for several poets here, and the magical realism of Mexico and Latin America is closely connected to the work of Ana Castillo. Jim Sagel has adopted local Spanish vernacular as a vehicle for his bilingual poetry. His work derives from New Mexico's language as well as its myths and customs. Jimmy Santiago Baca writes of and from his Chicano identity. The Language School, with its emphasis on a pure form, influences Arthur Sze and Mei-mei Berssenbrugge. And the poetry of Asia—particularly the distilled clarity of classical Chinese and Japanese poets—may be seen in the emphasis on image in the work presented here.

The geography of New Mexico is important to the nourishment of its poets. In an unusual synergy, one particular place in New Mexico has inspired two long poems by two very different poets. The healing shrine of the Santuario de Chimayó triggered both Martin Edmunds and Demetria Martinez to break out of the usual lyric bounds into the long poem or play. Edmunds returns to classical sources as venerable as Chaucer for the idea of a pilgrimage; for Martinez, it is as if the very earth begins to speak and to take on the identities of women buffeted by fortune.

The cities along the Rio Grande—Taos, Albuquerque, Santa Fe, and Las Cruces—are all vital centers of activity, each with its own style. Taos, for example, is currently famous for its wild "stand-up" style, in part inspired by its annual Poetry Circus, while in Las Cruces poets such as Denise Chávez write from the perspective gained by living near the border. In addition to the paradoxes brought about by living in a tourist town and the continuous intercultural dialogue, much of the work coming out of Santa Fe today is focused on women's themes. And in Albuquerque, eclecticism reigns, spurred by the ongoing readings by poets from throughout the state, the country, and the hemisphere, sponsored by the university and bookstores such as the Living Batch and Salt of the Earth.

Numerous New Mexico poets also live quietly in the hinterlands and remain relatively unaffected by city life. Nora Naranjo-Morse, for example, cannot be considered exclusively either a Santa Clara Pueblo or a Santa Fe poet; her work has an inner integrity not based solely on location. Carol Moldaw brings echoes of Boston and New York to work written in the village of Pojoaque, halfway between Santa Fe and Española.

New Mexico poets are sometimes influenced by a wide variety of seemingly disparate influences. For instance, Alvaro Cardona-Hine, living in the mountains of Truchas, combines influences as far-flung as his native Costa Rica, Japanese haiku, the lively Minneapolis poetry scene, and his own sensibility. He, like many others, is assuredly a New Mexico poet, having lived and worked here for years, but not solely of this soil. In contrast are the native New Mexico poets living in "exile" but continuing to produce writing related to this place—Leroy Quintana in San Diego, E. A. Mares in Texas, and Demetria Martinez in Tucson.

Where there are poets there is also publishing. *Puerto del Sol* magazine in Las Cruces has a long history of publishing New Mexico authors. *Blue Mesa Review* and the *Taos Review* are newer magazines in Albuquerque and Taos that present fresh work by local writers. John Brandi's Tooth of Time press has given many New Mexico poets a wider audience. And this anthology would not have been possible without the bibliographical guidepost of *New Mexico Poetry Renaissance: A Bibliography of Some Living Poets in the Collection of the Santa Fe Public Library* by Robert Winson, who is also the editor of *FishDrum* magazine.

If, as William Shakespeare said, the work of the poet is to give imagination "a local habitation and a name," then the poets of New Mexico have risen to the task.

Sharon Niederman and Miriam Sagan
Santa Fe, April 1994

L U C I L E   A D L E R

The Child at El Porvenir

"To this day, I treasure the photo of a child with a wreath of wild clover on her head, holding her father's hand under a giant pine tree at El Porvenir in the Gallinas Canyon, taken more than sixty years ago."

Born in Kansas City, Missouri, and educated at Bennington College, Lucile Adler lived in Cambridge, Massachusetts, for some years before settling with her family in Santa Fe. Her work has appeared in regional and national publications of note, including *The Nation*, *Poetry Northwest*, the *New Yorker*, *Puerto del Sol*, and *El Palacio*. Her books include *The Traveling Out* (MacMillan, 1967), *The Society of Anna* (Lightning Tree Press, 1974), and *The Ripening Light: Selected Poems 1977–1987* (Gibbs Smith, Publisher, 1989). She continues to live and write in Santa Fe.

"Since that first joyous encounter with New Mexico, I have explored some of its lives and landscapes and even have learned certain facts about its cultures and its past.

"But I remain a stranger—one who makes no claim to represent this complex and mysterious world in any literal way. It is here: it accepts our incursions generously; it offers noble spaces and grand shapes like Shiprock for us to contemplate with awe. Its secrets, to a degree, stay secret and intact.

"Though the light of New Mexico seems to permeate whatever I write, whether the setting is Santa Fe or Tibet, Canyon de Chelly or Akhmatova's Leningrad—and whether the heroine is Juniper Woman in her red shawl or Charlotte Brontë—I try to go beyond seductions of place to reach the interior horizons we all share.

"And I am still the child at El Porvenir who hopes her poems will seem to each of you to stand forth illuminated by what you already know."

AT THE CAVE MOUTH

Fires
Amber as eyes watching
Pine boughs burn
Lie down on the cave floor

A woman with oiled hair
A gentlewoman wrapped
In bloody hides and red fox fur
Stirs embers with a bone

Then opens her cloak to share
Nakedness
In the stone-cold dark
The first civility

Overhead
Painted gods
Hidden by night-smoke
Chase a red antelope

The woman blouses a child
At her bare breast
And enfolds a worn hunter
Glistening

Dreams

Oxblood polish on earth
Floors, flourish of horns
Through arches of rare wood
Where dyed flowers on wool

Hang at cold openings
Inventions   Civilities
Even love
Later

The fire lies down
And dies in the dark

Overhead
Warrior gods
Loose red spears and sleep
Unseen
Man and child
Swathed in silence
Sleep

At the cave mouth
Wakeful
Soul leaping white dawns
The woman chases
Tomorrow   alone

From the cave mouth
The sparks of her eyes
Look out

AFTER THE SIEGE OF LENINGRAD
(In World War II)

Akhmatova
wrote of a willow tree
in the snow

that was all

a young tree
alive still
in the ruins

so simple, so frail
grand, gay and free
she wept

longing to lead
the way beyond despair
at last

---

through silvery green
unimprisoned light
that could bend

like her heroic line
and rise, a small willow
in the snow or heroine

an Akhmatova, free
to heal silence

her profile a coastline
eroded but strong beside a distant sea

THE MESA WE CLIMBED

The mesa we climbed has no twin

Just as no light on pine tree or snow,
No face lit by love has a twin.

Together we discovered
Landscapes and seasons to live in
And part of us knows now,
Not how foreign they were,
But how it is to be foreign
Anywhere,

An alien stifled by silence,
Who must break out again
Into light unlike the sovereign
Light we climbed, must
Set out to find, neither
Escape route nor neighborhood—
But a calm level space,
A terrain like a green mesa top
Where new language might rise
With or without pine tree or
Snowlight or house; saying

Now you are gone, how it is
To be alien anywhere—
Saying, love,

The mesa we climbed has no twin.

J I M M Y   S A N T I A G O   B A C A

Poet of the Barrio

Photo: Michael O'Shaughnessy

"When I write, creating souls in my poems, I seem to see them rise as from a burning stick, some torch in the universe....Where does my poetry come from? I answer that I come from my poetry, I draw myself from poetry, I create myself from language, I sustain myself on poetry, I bear myself on poetry, I walk upright on two feet because of poetry."

Jimmy Santiago Baca was born in Santa Fe and grew up on the plains near the Manzano Mountains of New Mexico. His publications include *Immigrants in Our Own Land* (New Directions, 1993); *Black Mesa Poems* (New Directions, 1989); *Martín & Meditations on the South Valley* (New Directions, 1987), which won the American Book Award in 1988; and *Working in the Dark* (Red Crane Books, 1992).

"When I am at a backyard party with my friends, listening to Chicano music, and I see all these brown faces, young and old, spiritual euphoria permeates my being. My life becomes a celebration in honor of my people. They are a people who have suffered and worked and endured; whose stubborn reverence and love for life we call *corazón*. Perhaps that is why I write, to pay homage to my people and their ways."

Jimmy Baca has received a National Endowment for the Arts Creative Writing Fellowship for Poetry (1987) among other awards. He lives on a small farm beneath Black Mesa outside of Albuquerque with his wife Beatrice and his sons Antonio and Gabriel.

Quotations are from *Working in the Dark*.

EL GATO

At eight
El Gato's uncle lures them with grain in a pail
and shoots the brown pig between the eyes,
shoos the red-snouted white and black brothers
from guzzling blood in the trough.

At ten El Gato walks chop-block streets
with a rooster's tail strut
razored for a fight—life
a broken fire hydrant
flooding streets with blood.

In opulent estates,
fountains gazelle and bridal-train gardens drain
abundantly over spear-tipped walls.
Grecian statues offer laureled wisdom
to butlered adults with paper-weight hearts,
who answer the burning and gunning of America,
by building more prisons.

Nobody cares what El Gato'll find to eat or where he'll sleep,
under street lights throwing dirt clods
at hornets' nests, unafraid of being stung,
he vows to avenge his poverty,
to gash unmercifully with a bicycle chain
spineless attorneys taking advantage of his misery,
rob a construction executive in a limousine
sampling heroin off a hooker's thigh,
mug preppy brokers with golden smiles
whose gutter glares condemn him,
and all the chumps
who never cracked a soup-line biscuit
or had a court gavel crush their life,
should know he plans violent schemes against you,

prays
saints melt his pain red hot,
he'll hammer sharp to take you down
to darkness where he lives
and impale your heads

on La Virgen de Guadalupe's moon sickle.

Twelve years old. El Gato is no good,
dime bagging Peruvian flakes,
inhaling a glue-rag.
With all your police and prison sentences,
you can't chase El Gato from the street
or stop him from selling drugs,
because in his square white paper
lives God—El Gato deals God—who gives reprieve
from earthly hell and makes him feel good,
gives him hope and self-esteem,
and transforms despair to a cocaine-heaven,
until he's killed or OD's
like other homeboys trashed
on a stack of county jail corpses,
who understood life was a sewer grate
their dignity poured down with discarded litter,
where crack creates light when all one has is darkness.

Crack is God
when hopeless days bury El Gato under
rock piles of despair,
blocking him from feeling anymore,
breaking his heart into pieces of NOTHING.
El Gato is no good and preaches NOTHING door-to-door,
a strong kid full of NOTHING,
from NOTHING does he ask a blessing,
to NOTHING does he pray, hopes NOTHING
forgives his wrongs and NOTHING
helps when he takes vengeance on us.

Now fourteen,
beneath a moon above the sports caster's booth,
at the outdoors boxing coliseum,
after crowds go home and the ring removed,
El Gato shadowboxes invisible opponents
and raises his hand as champion.
El Gato joins homeboys against a rival gang,
skips bleachers over hand-rails out of breath,
and holds court in the field with bats, pipes, chains,
brass knuckles and guns,

in a game every kid has to hold a five-ace winning heart,
or die with a poker player's bluffing hand—
death nothing but an eight-ball roll on the break.

El Gato's life a Babe Ruth pop-up,
sailing beyond the rival gang's catch, hopscotching crime-
chalked sidewalks, fleeing police over backyard fences
from guard dogs barking,
down scuffed alleys where clapping windows and shutting
doors applaud him,
sliding under a stripped car home plate, hearing the news Jo-
Jo and Sparky got shot,
he x's their names off building scorecard-walls for dead.

At sixteen,
a brown fighting get down impromptu warrior,
lip-pursed ooohing fevered to defy,
clicking tap shoes on sidewalks,
chi chi chi cano, heel to toe, chin to chest,
chi chi chi cano,
T-shirt rolled to bare midriff, pomade hair back,
low-hugging hip khakis,
inked-cross on right hand,
bandanna'd, top button
tied on his Pendleton, lean and mean,
haunting us with his gangsta' signs.

El Gato learned his history
around water-bucket talk,
listening to mule-tongued growers
mutter holy whys they barbwired lands off,
clacking his hoe in grower's dirt
on skulls and bones of his people
murdered and buried in chains.
In branding-hot noon
he cuts lettuce for bronc-buckled
soft-palmed landowners
posing as frontiersmen,
their steer-horn Cadillac radios
tuned to religious broadcast
blaring glory to their godliness,
as they loom over him,

"God hates you spic. God hates you!
You're dirt, boy, dirt! Even dirt grows weeds,
but you, you're dirt that don't grow nothing but more dirt!"

Beat purple at nine,
wood-paddle whizzing
butt bullet stings.
El Gato touched washcloth to welted bruises
on thighs, legs, back, winced under the shower nozzle,
cursing life.
His heart the severed head of an outlaw
pickled in a jar of liquor and drugs
to numb the hurt.

Purging his shame for being born,
OD'd, was stabbed and shot,
wanting to believe he was bad.
It was better than falling into darkness
where nothing existed but more darkness.
El Gato wanted to exist even as dirt, no good dirt.

At nineteen, trying to rebuild his life,
El Gato got the urge to get high and did—
put pistol to his head and played roulette,
his bloodshot drunkard's eye seething rage
his guardian angel didn't want him dead.

The dirt yard pleads for his daughter's laughter,
her tricycle treads scribble,
You are always gone,
in whiskey and drugs,
never here to play or help me grow.

No heat, light or food.
His baby's crying
chisels on the headstone of his bones
her need for a father,
wobbles to a stop
when he picks her from the crib,
inhales her milky aroma,
patting and kissing her,
walking her back and forth

in the cold living room,
warming her in his skin heat,
breathing warmth on her,
holding her to his chest,
humming a deep-chest hymn
learned from his grandmother—
"Bendito, bendito, bendito sea dios,
los angeles cantan y daban a dios…"

"Blessed, blessed, blessed is the lord
the angels sing and give to the Lord…"
Her tiny hand flexes, a wing
unwrinkling from cocoon for flight,
fossilized in the stone of his arms.
El Gato is two men with one life—
he loves her, cares about her feelings,
wants to live at home, be a family man,
grow old with one woman.
But the warrior bares thorny teeth
at domesticity, slurs in disgust
at the dreamer's naiveté,
wants to brawl unafraid of dying young.

Tonight his infant is him
and he is her. He sees himself
as he was born,
innocent and perfect, whole life ahead of him,
and sees she can become him,
no good. He hums her holding tight,
melting into one hug humming her
'til dawn thaws frost down window casements
into stucco cracks, stray hounds croon in ruts,
yeowling cold from jaws, tooth-scratching
stickers from paws, he walks and walks
his sleeping infant in his arms,
humming hurting-man blues.

Thinking how to give his family a better life,
he strolls the ditch-bank next morning,
surprised to see pebbles last night's rain uncovered—blues
and greens. He wants his tears to reveal
what is covered in him like that.

He throws a stone in the irrigation water,
where it gasps his child's awe-struck mouth glistens
for breath, for a chance at life, glimmering ripples calling
him to be a father.
El Gato realizes he must start today.
Where the stone hits is the center of the ripples,
where the stone hits is the center that causes action. Where
the stone hits is the beginning,
where he is now,
is the center. He is the stone, he held in his hand as a kid
and threw to see how far it could go.

El Gato changed.
At twenty-one
he prayed
his lightning self
carve from thrown away wood-pile days
a faith
cut deep to the knot-core of his heart,
giving him a limb-top buoyancy
awakening, a realization that he was
a good man, a good human being,
healing emotional earthquakes in himself.

MEI-MEI
BERSSENBRUGGE

A Map of the Poem

Mei-mei Berssenbrugge was born in Beijing, China, in 1947. She grew up in Massachusetts and now lives in Santa Fe, New Mexico, with her husband, the sculptor Richard Tuttle, and their daughter Martha.

"I gather notes, quotations, pictures, and images, and construct a 'map' of the poem on a big table," Berssenbrugge says of her working process. "I write the first draft over five or six very intense days. Revisions are extensive, laborious, and slow."

Her books include *The Heat Bird* (Burning Deck, 1986) and *Empathy* (Station Hill Press, 1988). She has received two American Book Awards as well as the PEN West Award. Her most recent collection is *Sphericity* (Kelsey Street Press, 1993).

The long lines of her work, which fill the entire page, derive in part from a view of the New Mexico horizon line: vast and seemingly limitless.

CHINESE SPACE

First there is the gate from the street, then some flowers inside the wall,
then the inner, roofed gate. It is a very plain wall, without expressionistic
    means,
such as contrasting light on paving stones inside the courtyard to the
    calligraphed foundation stones.
My grandfather called this the façade or Baroque experience, rendering a
    courtyard transparent.
The eye expecting to confront static space experiences a lavish range of
    optical events,
such as crickets in Ming jars, their syncopation like the right, then left,
    then right progress
into the house, an experience that cannot be sustained in consciousness,
    because
your movement itself binds passing time, more than entering directs it.

A red door lies on a golden mirror with the fascinating solidity and
    peacefulness of the pond
in the courtyard, a featureless space of infinite depth where neither
    unwanted spirits nor light
could enter directly from outside. It lies within the equally whole space of
    the yard
the way we surrounded our individuals, surrounded by a house we could
    not wholly
retain in memory. Walking from the inner gate across a bridge which
    crossed four ways
over the carp moat, turning right before the ice rink, we pass roses
    imported from Boston,
and enter the main courtyard, an open structure like a ruin. This is not
    remembering,
but thinking its presence around eccentric details such as a blue and white
    urn turned up to dry,
although certain brightnesses contain space, the way white slipcovered
    chairs with blue seams contain it.

The potential of becoming great of the space is proportional to its distance
    away from us,
a negative perspective, the way the far corner of the pond becomes a
    corner again as we approach
on the diagonal, which had been a vanishing point. The grandmother poses
    beside rose bushes.

That is to say, a weary and perplexing quality of the rough wall behind her
    gives a power of tolerance
beyond the margins of the photograph. Space without expansion,
    compactness without restriction
make this peculiar and intense account of the separable person from her
    place in time,
although many families live in the partitioned house now. The reflecting
    surface of the pond
should theoretically manifest too many beings to claim her particular status
    in the space,
such as a tigerskin in space.

After the house was electrically wired in the thirties, he installed a ticker
    tape machine connected
to the American Stock Exchange. Any existence occupies time, he would
    say in the Chinese version,
reading stock quotations and meaning the simplicity of the courtyard into a
    lavish biosphere,
elevating the fact of its placement to one of our occupation of it, including
    the macaw speaking Chinese,
stones representing infinity in the garden. This is how the world
    appears when the person
becomes sufficient, i.e., like home, an alternation of fatigue and relief in the
    flexible shade of date trees,
making the house part of a channel in space, which had been interior, with
    mundane fixtures
as on elevator doors in a hotel, a standing ashtray that is black and white.
The family poses in front of the hotel, both self-knowing and knowing
    others at the same time.
This is so, because human memory as a part of unfinished nature is
    provided
for the experience of your unfinished existence.

SPHERICITY

1

Emphasizing not only the ground upon which her movement builds, but
matter it forms, the idea
of movement is a material, also, like the transparency of light above a blue
ridge *being* apricot,
though the ridge is not the blue color of air on it. This light like a space
that's a passage
in time. There's movement when the space changes and in its state of being
what it changed to.
The content of your focus on it, like an image, can start suddenly. The way
my eye makes the horizon,
my state of mind is making the state of being of the space. The state of
mind touches an object
by watching it against graduated lines in a reflection. "The ridge grows
bluer," instead of coordinating
a change from patches of contacts. The mystery of a color can diminish
without the ridge becoming opaque.
Every other moment of an experience must push to extravagance or
sphericity, of horizon, not magnitude.

2

The time of having her becomes an absorptive surface, instead of when the
person was alive.
There was an inseparable light of the event for each place, like a birthplace.
The horizon
represented a passage in time *and* light, a one way membrane she thinks is
the edge of a shadow,
like a medical procedure into her body. Then, color crosses back from a
petal. I can correlate
my sensation of reddening with changes in the sky. I can't graph my sense
of this position of my body,
which has no degree, but is more like time on either side of you. Each point
of the space
marks the center of a sphere, as if your eyes were a point. As if a person
being were like hearing.
Her time is the center of increasing disorder, an arrow in space.

3

It is finite in extent, yet has no edges, like the surface of the earth. On the
    horizon,
an apricot seam is not the content of a concept of you. Knowing this light,
    like knowing home,
is not a content, but seeing it is a content of my consciousness. If it's an
    image, it
can have content, i.e., telling something to me, or if you were telling the
    content of your dream.

4

The image of an apricot band of light in my memory, does not block out
    the impression of this band,
now. I can see your shoes on red dirt that covers blue hills and the pulsating
    band turn redder.
I define red by pointing to dirt, not like the shadow of a petal, a place in
    time, not a thing
with closeness or distance, as if I were walking instead of looking or
    remembering. The use I speak
of seeing is a form of use. Light releases events and things away from the
    thing to the culture
of the person or presence, as if a pivot between the necessity of relation
    among human beings,
called agreement in the form of life, and the lack of this necessity between
    time and a collapsed star.

JOHN BRANDI

Where Heart, Mind, Myth, Rock, and Mirage Overlap

"Since 1971 I have made New Mexico my home, drawn to its landscape because it matches an interior one—a convergence of dream and reality with an ever-present edge of heightened awe....There is something of my personality in the land's shape and color, in the brilliant, quiet light of solitude, in the sharpness of edge meeting edge, sky cutting apart earth. The desert speaks with the ideal language of a poem: emotionally charged, alive with mystery and surprise—a topography bathed in light, christened with sudden shadows, full of passionate syllables, landforms rising and falling with little predictability.

"New Mexico is a good place to come back to after venturing into other landscapes that call me: the arid backshadow of the Himalayas, the Arctic desert, the peaks of the San Juan, the Ring of Fire."

John Brandi began painting and writing as a child, inspired by travels with his parents. Born in 1943, he remembers early sojourns into the Mohave Desert, Sierra Nevada, and Big Sur , as well as a train ride through the Great Basin to the Great Lakes. Then there was always a return to the "garden"—his Los Angeles backyard lush with hibiscus, citrus, magnolia, narcissus, and poinsettia. With the Peace Corps in the 1960s, he organized Quechua land rights unions in highland Ecuador and began publishing on an ancient mimeo machine inked with used crankcase oil. In the Upper Amazon, he lived with a healer and delivered his poems by raft to the local post office. Travel, family life, and building a remote cabin in the Sangre de Cristos, where he lived seven years, followed. His press, Tooth of Time, devoted its efforts to printing unpublished poets. Many broadside, mimeo, and letterpress sheets he sewed by hand or stitched on an old Singer treadle machine.

For the past two decades, John has followed the trail of itinerant poetry gigs in Alaska, Montana, New Mexico, California, New York, and Nevada—

"urban and hinterland, elderly and incarcerated, ranchers, Navajo Nation, Yupik people." His recent journeys have taken him to Java, Komodo, Sumbawa, Flores. He has received "a few" awards—Witter Bynner, Djerassi Foundation, PEN American Center, and National Endowment for the Arts, but the real rewards he considers "loving children and an expanding garden— amaranth, girasol, datura, jalapeños, basil, and tomato."

His books include *Desde Alla* (Tree Books, 1971), *Chimborazo: Life on the Haciendas of Highland Ecuador* (Akwesasne Notes, 1976), *Diary from a Journey to the Middle of the World* (The Figures, 1979), *Poems at the Edge of Day* (White Pine, 1984), *That Back Road In* (Wingbow Press, 1985), *Hymn for a Night Feast* (Holy Cow!, 1988), *In the Desert We Do Not Count the Days* (Holy Cow!, 1991), *Shadow Play* (Light & Dust, 1992), *Weeding the Cosmos* (La Alameda Press, 1994). Upcoming books are *Heartbeat Geography: Selected & Uncollected Poems* and *A Question of Journey: The Asia Diaries*. Brandi makes his home in Corrales, New Mexico, where he also sells his paintings.

"As the spirit of the landscape—wherever it may be—enters the flesh and is made portable, it becomes humanized, finds dwelling, and sings out again through the mouth. Thus, a poem. Not of the mind, but of the body. Octavio Paz said, 'Eternity depopulates the instant.' If so, poetry repopulates it. Charges it with raw, forceful gesture. Walking through the world, whether it be that of one's own backyard garden, sidewalk barrio, or river woods, or that of the planet's vast ghettos, deserted oceans, spoiled forests, unconquerable spires, or underwater reefs—the poem is 'given' as is given a sudden feast.

"We walk, yet constantly fall within the dream called life. Flowers are gathered, a bouquet forms in the hand. Some of the flowers are wild, others cultivated—hybrid. Short poems are tiny corollas flaring with an aftershock of color. Long poems have lengthy stamens shaped to charm the bee—or sphinx moth. They all have a place, and a pleasing arrangement cannot happen without attention to dissimilarities. I never hope for a perfect bouquet. What I love is the excitement of the senses through fusion and juxtaposition. Mix of color. Gleanings that know no political, cultural, or psychological boundary."

I SAW KIT CARSON STILL ALIVE

*"He was a likable soft-spoken man
whose exploits contributed much toward
the settlement of the West."*
—Encyclopedia Britannica

I saw Kit Carson still alive
cruising the reservation, driving through Window Rock
up over the hill towards Naschitti and Biklabito,
the consumer producer vending obsolescence
measuring people in units of profit
reading the desert as one vast printout.

I saw him step from an Eagle,
the BIA official from back east, looking for points
to advance his career. He was the relocation agent
eyeing hillsides, surveying canyons, planning
quick-development housing, calling long distance
to line up friends for under-the-table contracts.

I watched him at Black Mesa.
I saw him at Shiprock, pulling the brake at
Colonel Sanders, cleaning his carbine
on a formica table, bulldozing peach trees
handing out free radioactive mine tailings
telling the people of Paguate, "Here, make your adobes
build new foundations."

He was in Tohatchi and Many Farms,
marching school kids through freezing rain
to salute the flag. He was holed up in a town
named after Cortez, the liquor retailer
sitting up late designing billboards
showing a tight-jeaned woman beckoning men
with an open blouse and outstretched arm
holding a bottle of tokay.

He swiveled in his chair, downshifted into third
rode a glass elevator high above the world
three thousand miles away.
I saw him slip into his saddle, unfold his maps

spit dust outside Paradise Disco
pass out Bibles under a portable placard saying:
First Indian Free Will Full Gospel Pre-
Millennium Church of God.

He cocked his hat, timed his watch;
his infrared cigarette burned down into the night.
He talked low, made camp
built a hogan-shaped saloon
with his brother-in-law a hundred yards
from the reservation boundary.

He was the one who grabbed Mrs. Yazzie
by her velveteen collar
and pushed her into the snow when she came to save
her husband from another night of drinking.

I saw him, Kit Carson
working gears and levers way up high
behind the scoop of his three-million dollar
power shovel, training men to dig up the land
trade in the old ways, mine coal, get a job
with Sacred Mountain Electric.

He was the powerplant industrialist
breaking for lunch at Best Western Inn.
He polished his spurs, got a shave, had a girl sent up
to his room. He was there generating sulfurous haze
over cornfields and rivers, spilling waste
into drinking holes and village wells.
He was busy manufacturing electricity for Los Angeles
and Phoenix, the gambling halls of Vegas
the used-car lots and nuke sites.

I saw him down low
behind the tinted windows of his Cougar
secretly jotting notes for his Ph.D., writing a book
to size things up; in Tuba City, in Round Rock
he was there bribing Indian leaders
buying off tribal officials
to pave inroads for corporate bosses to confuse
the Athapaskan grandmother and steal her land.

He was getting rich on radioactive disposal
on Pampers, on Lethal 1080 used to wipe out Coyote.

He kicked dust from his hooves
climbed Defiance Plateau in his four wheeler
had a picnic at Washington Pass, looking down into
wide expanse of red desert and brown mesas
he spied through field glasses
and licked his chops.

On the highways,
in the bars   —it was 1864 1878 1964 1989.
I saw Kit Carson,
        he was still there, doing his thing.

THIS LANGUAGE ISN'T SPEECH

This language isn't speech.
It's a blossom in the doorway slowly opening;
one reverberation
        mating with another—heat of a rose,
salt smoke from a sea wave.
Something inside the flesh that trembles
            as the center shifts between us.

It is very quick isn't it?

This montage of soundwaves
describing silence. Question mark inscribed
in a storm of pollen.

I give you a floating island,
one eye to see, another to feel. You arch your back,
shake gold leaf into a shower of Off Minor.

This language is a horizon
terraced into a ladder that spins
into a blade of light, and drugs the darkness
                    with its brilliant stem.

Desire smiles in all directions at once.

It's the magnet in your pocket.
It's two minerals in their proper field of glow.
It's the summer tanager in silver chamisa.
It's your handprint in the sun
    bringing forth the names of children.

Think of wings pushing through shoulders.
Think of drinking the compass to become a map.
Think of rain pouring from an eave
with no cloud above, a wet alphabet trembling
inside the spine. Or to escape through the letter O
        to be naked inside the curve of an S.

You're the symbol for what you write.
Pumpkin blossom, dewdrop, mica;
a stone-pecked bird inside the chest
        of a star-headed man.
You're the barefoot girl in a mirrored cove
who trims the leaves and greets the sun.
You're a cyclone breathing phosphorescence
            into space between the hands
                thirsting at the gate.

You open the door, I see you part way
        —taste the jazz of what's begun,
form a lasso of stars   and laugh
that you are real—that webs of blood and crystal
begin what we speak   or that what we speak
is more like silk ... slowly sliding back and forth
over two bodies undressed in the stillness
    there in the shine,
            there   very deep.

Adventure does not drive me.
Nor reason. Something in the genes
alchemically combines with impulse
and sets forward the feet—into thin flint-scented air,
        oxygenless realm of creaking stone
            large-knuckled pillars of ice.

Heights constantly change,
loss of gravity challenges my grip.
This flesh I wear is of the slow-paced race,
awkward in vertical trudge over ancient reefs
and fossil shorelines once skimmed
by ancestral fin
        in horizontal glide.

Ultimately I accept the thin air,
feed on stellar equations, thrive on endless designs
of bronze and violet inside the eye.
Body is a walking sutra, skull throbs
with storm, ancestral memory
           —seeds of the unborn.

Lao Tzu's poems are agates in a tarn.
   Bodhi Dharma's meditation wall, a glacial face
mottled with debris. Mirabai's bangles,
      frost breaking mountains into shards.

And my erratic breathing,
primal wheeze and heave
of dissonant vocabulary: something
of the mother tongue, rudder of song, heatwave
in a field of ice—a chant far from mind
          deep in the Blood Garden of the body.

Spectator, participant,
I am the face of everything seen:

Behind a weathered pole-frame ladder (a village
reminiscent of New Mexican pueblos) a stately woman
in Tibetan dress combs out her shimmering hair to dry.

Around a corner, a sudden lump of soiled rags
warms itself in crisp high-altitude sun:
an old man—forlorn, mouth caked with spittle,
eyes shut with mucous.   He can't see but knows I'm here.
Knows my race, my transience.   And waves me away.
Above him, looms the mountain's crystal presence.
            Anna   —sustenance.
                        Purna —goddess.

Stranger here, stranger
back home—I walk to call things by name,
rid of accumulation and regain perspective.
To wander is to own nothing, become small
in the shadow of a massif larger,
more mysterious than anything dreamed.

If there by duty connected with this journey
it is to give significance to it.
To ascend each switchback, not by foot
            but by power of a humble song.

Cold, soaked with sweat,
I absorb the sunrise: violet-green atmosphere
    short breaths   small steps
5-7-5 ledge-to-ledge leaps
            6/8 improvisational circumam-
bulation around a whitewashed cairn
whose fluttering prayer flags
            transform wind into mantra.

Nomad. Harvester.
The body traverses solidified fire,
sunlight webbed in chlorophyll veins, lichen scrolls,
micaceous glitter untamed in vertical folds.
Home is exactly this place I stand,
alphabets planted wherever tracked
    —grain and chaff carried in cuff
            or glued to the sweat of the sole.

The pass is in the heart.
We shall always be crossing it, acclimatizing,
gauging the slope.

Time halts at the summit,
becomes a concentric ripple inside the eye.
When it opens, it opens
with the very first moment of the world.
In it, I'm simply here, a concentrated semblance
set to flame.   Truth is beauty, the elemental reality
that surrounds. Doubt is that ragged gap
flushed with sunlight, through which I've hiked.

From peak to peak, snow banners
feed infinity fine sparkles of jeweled dust.
It is here that I begin.
Humble and pedestrian,   at crest
                —becoming light with the climb.

ALVARO
CARDONA - HINE

Photo: Lin Eagle

The Delectable Fruits of Silence

Born in San José, Costa Rica, Alvaro Cardona-Hine has lived most of his life in the United States. A self-taught artist, he actively practices three disciplines: musical composition, writing, and painting. His poetry has appeared in over sixty literary magazines. Cardona-Hine is the author of eleven books of poetry and prose and recipient of a National Endowment for the Arts fellowship. He lives in Truchas, New Mexico, where he exhibits his work in the Cardona-Hine Gallery.

"I have no working process that I can recognize or describe," he says. "Each day is a tree of verbal apples one may climb or stone at will. I am usually up there, unless I am after the even more delectable fruits of silence."

number five

when I think I have met the oldest
man   I meet yet another   this one
tottering   this one naturally
blaming his wife's
skirt   literally
keeping the gravestone
cooling

they walk toward me   they wave
from cars driven by that other lady
I am leaning on my shovel
and they pass laughing
having gone from bad
to worse on a day's
notice

they build nothing   they have stopped
what started with drinking

one of them walks in circles
because it gives him
nothing to do

it's like that here   a kingdom
of dissolute humor
where something Spanish
turns out to be blood
on Christ's knee
as when old man Padilla
wants back a tool
he never lent me

number six

the young ones   on the other hand   came
to build my house from spit and piss

came in droves   needing money for booze
if no wife was home
to claim it first

from them I learned bargains are
paid with laughter   which ends
when they overdose
three days before the preachers
preach them dead

this is my illegitimate brood   blessing
and disaster   in the midst of a hymn
to altitude I want to stop the sun
and have it build us the better
house   ah but sunshine is only paint
it goes well on walls
when the painter is about

night   or one of these deaths
has the feel of the now sinister
forest   where Egyptian eyes
on the trunks of the aspen
look and never blink

this passage as into wax   this
situation between living and dead
in unlabeled bottles
contains the future and the young
as if they were grasshoppers
set to jumping
from coffin to coffin
in the parched fields
of Hell

number eleven

here the cemeteries
plunge
down the mountain
one is sure to be
buried
standing for rigor mortis

if you are a member
of this or that clan
you'll have a backyard
full of plastic flowers
below the open beak
of the Sangres

those who can afford it
celebrate dying with taffeta skirts
with the lips of lilies

the poor
are buried in some socket
of ignorance

ignorant
until the last minute
when they let out a scream

it's such a relief to die
when you have given birth
to so much that is
nothing

number twenty-three

they knew how to farm beans
among unyielding rock
in the upper reaches
beyond the llano where at noon
wild turkeys call
as if the earth were young

the Los Alamos atom brought
jobs and ideas   the priest
was sent for a twelve pack
perfect

the old grannies who sat
in their doorways
puffing at lavender ecstasy

were replaced
custom is to have a hacking
cough   loud and insolent

what was right   the wall-bending
families among the pigs the goats
all gone the way of the fix

no rooster crows   even the cows
are dishonest   money came
the wars went and burned
the wedding photos

distrust is the edge
of politeness   only the very
old   the tottering blind like a burning
can show you on God's shoulder
where the furrows went

to go to church
one pries open
the legs of the prostitute

number twelve

those geraniums
fool no one   this is a town
where all the curtains
have them looking at each
other   staring across an empty street
full of dogs   drunks
on crutches   oh

when the stranger comes
and he's new   like an
angel or a toy   the paisley
shivers   the breeze
dials gossip green
the cronies laugh

the stranger's here

to be devoured
look at him   birds of darkness
look at him beginning to dissolve
in your suspicious gullet

let him taste you also
let him get back at you
from his window   let him
destroy you with his distant thunder
his fear of having crawled up your wall
like a beetle

ANA CASTILLO

Photo: Robert Birnbaum / Stuff Magazine

The Particularities of New Mexico

Ana Castillo is a poet, novelist, essayist, editor, and translator. Her poetry collections include *My Father Was a Toltec: New and Collected Poems* (W. W. Norton & Company, 1994) and *Women Are Not Roses* (Arte Público Press, 1984). Her novels include *So Far from God* (W. W. Norton & Company, 1993), *The Mixquiahuala Letters* (Doubleday & Company, 1992), and *Sapogonia* (Doubleday & Company, 1994).

"I am very fascinated by the particularities of New Mexico. The one thing that New Mexicans have, native New Mexicans that have been there for generations, is a great sense of land and space. They have land on which seven or eight generations have been buried. And to meet, particularly what I would refer to as Chicanas, who could say, 'my great-great-great-great-grandparents were buried here, and this is my land and I have two hundred and fifty acres or two hundred acres' blows me away, being a city gal from Chicago. You know, because we get moved around by urban renewal every few years or so. But I'm also first-generation Mexican, and my family comes from a very humble background, so the Spanish was familiar to a degree."*

Castillo holds a Ph.D. in American Studies from the University of Bremen, FRG, an M.A. in Latin and Caribbean Studies from the University of Chicago, and a B.A. from Northeastern Illinois University. Her awards and grants include the Carl Sandburg Literary Award in Fiction, a New Mexico Arts Commission Grant, and a National Endowment for the Arts Poetry Fellowship.

"Neruda said that your home is where your books are. And so I did find a place where I can keep my books; my books stay there, so my books have a home."*

Castillo has a house in Albuquerque, New Mexico.

YOU ARE REAL AS EARTH, Y MÁS

I

A green chile ristra
you are, 'manito—
hung upside down,
on a rustic porch.
Rock, you are,
coyote, roadrunner,
scorpion stung
still running strong. Sometimes,
you are a red ristra
into whom I take burning bites
and always yearn for one
more
bite.
You are real as earth y más.
You are air and sky. While I—
who have travelled so far to reach you,
remain the blood of fertility,
fear of your mortality,
pungent waters in which
you believe, you will surely
die a godless death.

II

And when you are not sky,
nor warm rain,
nor dust or a pebble in my shoe,
you are the smoke
of an old curandera's cigar
trailing throughout my rooms.
You are the Warrior Monkey
in a Chinese Buddhist tale; you are
copper and gold filigree—
Tlaquepaque glass blown
into the vague shape of a man,
a jaguar, a gnat. I
look for signs to see if it is really you.
Tonantzín appears as Guadalupe
on a burnt tortilla.
Coffee grounds, wax, an egg dropped

into a clear jar of water.
I look for signs everywhere.

III
I have lit farolitos to guide
you back to my door.
Turned upside down by desire,
it seems your feet
are on a groundless path. Beware of the Trickster.
The road in either direction
is neither longer nor shorter,
nor more narrow nor wider
than the fear that closes your heart.
Grey ash sediment in my entrails,
this path of ours is Sacred Ground.

YOU FIRST

Seems like a long time
since i let a man
make me a promise
longer still
since i believed in one.

But there is room
in this house
of our childhood
to convene once again.

Its green wall kitchen
perennial beans and comal
on the stove. The oil base
painted bedrooms
small living room
t.v. console, altar
in the corner by the door.

A house where men watched
in secret as i undressed

and a life of Friday to Friday
paychecks.

"Don't open the door
for your cousin Manuel—
who just got out of the pinta."
Two nights later
on the news
he is shot
robbing a liquor store.

A house of closed doors and men
not to be trusted.

So here we are, you and i. You,
wanting a second chance:
"What d'you say, little sister?"
Being the gambling woman i am
i draw for the highest card.

Don't trust men: not a poet
with his Cortes' lust for words.
Not an artist who'll paint
you away.

Don't trust men of the world
nor those who have no use for it.

But in this house where you recall
a girl's burgeoning breasts
i played with dolls
pressed your khakis
dusted your room
during your Army days.

i now can say—
i would have killed you gladly then
a clean blow to the neck

wanting me
wanting me
breathing me through a red eyed glare.

An Ace will beat all. i'll walk off
as i have in so many dreams:
913 South Miller, Taylor St., Chicago.

It's either you or me.
i can't leave,
not the daughter.

There must be room in this house
where on Christmas Eve i clumsily
smother dough on corn leaves,
and if you ask—
serve your coffee.

It's the luck of the draw, big brother.

We've both done too much time,
both made of the stuff
that never relents.
i leave it
to a small square deck,
crimped and handled
from too many crooked plays.

i won't say no, but i won't say yes.
i'll only say: you first.

THE ROAD TO ZACAPO

A young man I hardly knew
came by.
And in that off-handed way
of cocky young men,
who don't have a cent,
won't shave
going to a woman's home—
look around unimpressed,
drink her liquor,
eat her food,

leave the plate on the table,
take a nap on her couch
knowing
she has things to do—
stayed two days.

When it was dark, he asked
if I believed in God,
and whether or not he had satisfied
me in bed. At midnight he left
to see a girl
who waited for him.

And, as if all that he had taken
and all that I had given
were not enough—
He asked for a poem
just for him:

On the road to Zacapo
tío Carmen
machete in hand,
stops before daybreak
to eat tortillas
tía Luz has made.
No one disturbs tío Carmen,
although the machete, he says,
is only for clearing the path.

I remember you, "Ojos de chocolate,"
tu mata de pelo negro,
tío Carmen en Michoacán.
Nothing is past, a story already told,
a fate fixed to a defeat.
You don't remind me of anyone, as you feared,
and yet—you are all the places I've seen,
and those where I've yet to be:
Zacapo,
East L.A.,
Chicago barrio.
Tijuana, where your grandfather
proselytizes against sin,

a winding, reckless train to Mexico City, 1963.
I am 10 years old and thirsty.

I am a godless woman who prays for you.
Ademas, de pilón
te regalo estos versos—
to wish you light,
to find your way,
and sometime soon, if you like,
back to me,
back to me.

DENISE CHÁVEZ

The Words behind Closed Doors

"I write poetry because when I was growing up my mother was fearful when I closed my bedroom door. She was a woman who wanted our house to be open: no secrets. But everyone has to have secrets, especially children. I began writing in diaries because I always needed to close my personal door. Those diaries became notebooks first of other people's poems and then eventually of mine. One day I realized all the words in my notebook were mine! What a blessing words are—to close doors, open them at will, and to attempt to understand why we have secrets."

Poet, playwright, novelist, and teacher, Denise Chávez lives in her hometown of Las Cruces. Her newest book is *Face of an Angel* (Farrar, Straus and Giroux, 1994). Her plays have been produced throughout the United States and Europe, including performances at the Edinburgh Festival and the Festival Latino de Nuevo York, through Joseph Papp. Among her awards are a National Endowment Inter-arts Grant, 1982, a Rockefeller Foundation Fellowship, and the Favorite Teacher Award from the University of Houston, where she taught theater for five years. She has worked extensively with Very Special Arts, the visually handicapped, prison populations, and the elderly.

LEGAÑA OF LACE

Manina: great aunt
hunched, wall-eyed
with recriminations.

A tatter of mantilla
hung chainlike
from the corner of her eye
a dried thing
stained, crusted with sleep
vapors of grace
expectation
and the flowing to the other side.

Jordan is a land of mercy.
Texas is a land of what?

Your rosary is a small dark dream
it is faded cloth
it is tired with the death of passion
soft, with acceptance.

She fingered it.
Legaña.

The shell turned inward
the mountains turned outward
their waist of blue
encircled majesty
their razored silhouette
of purple labial sky, opened,
tender.

She fingered it.
The weeds too real
the mountains a cutout,
and out of dream.

So, I equate an old woman's prayers
with the edge of lace run through
an old glassed eye staring out

proceed to mountain
sky
and close with space.

MERCADO DAY

Mercado	Day
Mango	Day
Asadero	Day
Blood Sausage	Day

We sit in the car
doors opened
hanging out of the seats
peeling skin of mango fruit
joyous
without words
eating

Mother in front
Father in back
me at the wheel

We just finished our lunch
asadero
blood sausage
avocados
¿Cuáles están listas?
tortillas de maíz
las de de veras

Shivering dripping hands
lift Orange Fantas, Sprites and ice cold Cokes
from the dispenser in the center aisle
paid Mariachis
serenade us
with *Guadalajara*
tierra quemada

as the shoe shine boys
with their shiny wooden boxes
perch on the stairway
watching us eat

Wet sticky hands
cannot wipe away
last traces
of this last holy meal
the parking lot
receptacle of our remains

I drive through Juárez
confident
safe
"I understand the way Mejicanos drive—
they drive like me"

I am not afraid
it is when I leave
the terror begins

Mercado Day
Mango   Day
Asadero Day
I recalled that feast
years later
in the rain

Mother is dead
and Father will never drive again

I step on the gas
I'm not afraid
I understand the way Mejicanos drive—
Joyous
singing
Guadalajara
tierra quemada

¡Aguacates!
¡Queso fresco!

Dulces de camote
Mother's favorites
los míos de bizñaga
Ande, Señorita
Ssst!   Hey lady!
You wanna buy?

Después
later
later
I say

Mercado	Day
Mango	Day
Asadero	Day
Blood Sausage	Day

ARTERY OF LAND

Artery of land
the water flecks quench
certain
desert thirsts

Your pore-red valleys
wander
sun-paths
along the vision line
of that New Mexico heat

Small children remember
afternoons pricking them

Feigning sleep
in airless rooms

They recall
tiny beads of sweat:

Home.

JUDSON CREWS

Avant-Garde Renegade

Photo: Mildred Tolbert

"True, I have lived three-fifths of my life in New Mexico, but most of the New Mexico literary community would be indignant at the thought of my being embraced as a New Mexico poet."

Born in Waco, Texas, in 1917, Judson Crews received his B.A. and M.A. from Baylor University. Trained in sociology and psychology, after serving in the Army Medical Corps during World War II he journeyed to Big Sur and New York City, becoming part of the avant-garde literary and artistic scenes on the coasts. His book *Henry Miller and My Big Sur Days: Vignettes from Memory* (Vergin Press, 1992) is a frank, behind-the-scenes memoir, taken from his ten-thousand-page original account of time he spent in Miller's orbit. Like Miller, Crews took delight in ignoring the rules of censorship, participating in that impulse toward freedom which transformed American literature and culture forever.

He took these experiences with him to Taos, where he lived for two decades, editing and publishing many small magazines. His own writing has appeared in numerous publications, and in 1983 Ahsahta Press published his collection *The Clock of Moss*, edited and with an introduction by Carol Berge. He now resides in Albuquerque.

I AM STILL AS STONE

Beside this motionless glass
lake among naked peaks

One high eagle shifts barely
the serenity of his knowing glide

The landscape has altered—
it seems never unaltered

Either in the moment's perspective
or the ether he drifts upon—

The light changes, the air, the shape-
less clouds reshaping always

What may be beneath the lake
of depths—what is only reflection

Upon its glaze. Savages
peer with caution and care

And fear, into the rare quick-
silver surface in the explorer's hand

CLIMBING

To the petroglyphs over shale
and half-melted snow

Though the sun is bright
and the day is warm

I am thinking that I
cannot even read "buffalo"

A few cow chips mar
the way

I cannot read "holy" or "squaw"
an "arrow" may be the direction

Of the wind. But every one
knows "rain cloud"

Vultures float high
and quietly

Their language only
clear as my own

RETURNING TO TAOS,
    AFTER MANY SEASONS

Refusing to renew the unction of breathing
sharply in upon the air, to tackle

The bridle holding bay the central total
I sought the powder-maker's small

Purchase of survival, whacking sticks
in a small pile, reading them over

In an *I Ching* fashion, under the stars
of that high heaven as smoke curled up

The sharp frost came in upon us early
the woman poking me, saying we had to get

Up and go—she couldn't stand the cold. We
traced a trail I seemed to know before

VICTOR DI SUVERO

Photo: Barbara Windom

After a Lifetime with the Sea

Victor di Suvero was born in Italy in 1927, grew up in China, and emigrated with his family as political refugees to the United States in 1941.

"I first came to New Mexico in 1968. The vague mention of the Marranos who had come after the time of the Inquisition to this furthest frontier of the Spanish Empire stirred strange feelings in my spirit. It was the Inquisition that had driven my ancestors from Malaga up the coast and over to Padua and Venice where they settled five hundred years ago, and to realize that the waves of exile had come around from the other direction—closing the circle, girdling the globe, made me feel I had come home."

Di Suvero is the author of five collections of poetry, including *The San Francisco Poems* (The Pennywhistle Press, 1987) and *Tesuque Poems* (The Pennywhistle Press, 1993). He was the poetry editor of *Crosswinds Magazine* for three years and is the founder of the Poetry Center of New Mexico. He served on the board of directors of the National Poetry Association for five years and presented National Poetry Week in Santa Fe in 1990.

"This land had been the sea at one time. After a lifetime with the sea, another one in the high desert might extend my round of consciousness. But I have not abandoned the world I knew before coming to New Mexico. I have brought it with me as so many people do when they come here."

Di Suvero lives in "a house with bookshelves" in Tesuque, New Mexico.

TO LIVE WITH THE BELOVED

To live with the beloved
One does not rely solely
On mystic connections
The alembic dance of the flowers
The understandings of never before
The sweat of delight in the bed
The stillness of sunset
When the wind has died down
And there is food in the house.

To live with the beloved
One does not leap into
Dangerous waters, quicksand
Or otherwise risk life and soul
Without concern, play cards
With the devil, give up
Discourse, run with the crowd,
Retire into deserts and solitude
Or bark at the moon dismayingly.

To live with the beloved
One must learn to be up
With the dawn for its blessings
To wash dishes as sacrament
To clean the house in ways
That are luminous, to sing
And fetch and follow through and
Tend to the tangible maintaining
The body in balance with spirit.

Otherwise the days are numbered, the sand
Is measured out, the fabric tears, expressions
Ring hollow, the bud withers
And one is no longer there
At all.

WINTER SOLSTICE

This is the time when the great wheel
Of the year dips down
When the sun shines the trees
In the north at noon
When the deer's breath and the hare's breath
And the dog's cloud the still cold
With their small handfuls of steam
This is the time when the cross exists
Only in the outstretched arms
Of the winter's tree
And the child in each of us is born once more.

This is the time when the great wheel
Of the world dips down
When the wave's spume becomes ice
As the wind takes the salt drops to give them shape
For a moment before
Dropping them once again
Into the hard driving sea to melt.
This is the time when so many of those
Ready to die choose to go
Into the space between the stars
Where the dreams live
And the child in each of us is born once more.

This is the time when the great wheel
Of the stars dips down
When the Pleiades come close
And the Great Bear shines
When the summer's fruit
And the winter's grain join
In the faith that Spring will come
And be light again
This is the time that forgives the hurt
That sings and praises
And the child in each of us is born once more.

MARTIN EDMUNDS

Listening to Silence

"I came to New Mexico for the wind and the ocean of sky. This is an impassioned landscape. It wears, if not its heart, then at least its spilled blood on its sleeve," says Martin Edmunds. "When I first arrived, I wondered if my poems could get their tongues around the names on the land: Acequia Madre (mother ditch), the Sangre de Cristo Mountains. Would I come to taste in a name the clay of the place, would the winds of Taos, of Truchas, of Las Trampas whistle through my teeth when I speak of them?"

Edmunds was born in Waltham, Massachusetts, in 1955. He received his A.B. from Harvard University and went through the master's program in Creative Writing at Boston University. From 1986 to 1989 he was a Writing Fellow at the Cathedral of St. John the Divine in New York, where his short verse plays on the life of St. Francis of Assisi were produced.

"I was raised Catholic, so the fiestas here are not so different from the festas I was brought up on in Boston's North End," says Edmunds, "except that La Conquistadora was unknown to us. The Virgin turned a milder face when we prayed, calling 'Ma Donna' when she was paraded through the streets in a shipshape float hung with fishing nets."

Edmunds is the winner of the 1991 "Discovery"/*The Nation* contest. His manuscript *The High Road to Taos* was one of the 1993 National Poetry Series winners; it was published by the University of Illinois Press in the summer of 1994. His poetry has been anthologized in *Under 35: The New Generation of American Poets* (Doubleday & Company, 1989) and in the *Arvon Anthology* (Arvon Foundation, 1989).

"Writing is listening," he says, "and the courage to wait, however long it takes, for the right word to appear. This is why the best poems contain silence, contain time."

Edmunds lives in Pojoaque, New Mexico, with his wife, poet Carol Moldaw.

THE HIGH ROAD TO TAOS

I. Taos

Morning comes to life
with the grating of shovel and pick.
Wind shrills like a fife
in the reeds. Against the heraldic

escutcheon of sunrise
stands the red bull, black
as the shadow of the morada
that never dries.

Sharp stones, wind, thorns, and wild
water staring in puddles.
The Campo Santo huddles
its shoulders against the cold.

The Campo Santo sits
jostled among small hills.
Its tenants are done with dawn's
pink slips and unpaid bills.

They sleep. The starved eye feeds
on winter deaths, the red
dirt piled high above
each temporary bed.

Big-bellied, each fresh grave's
a woman giving birth.
When the meek inherit the earth,
this is the acre they get.

They have been carried across
the bridge that skims the river.
Their bodies were bathed in the front room,
their hearts in the Guadalquivir.

They have been carried across
the river and the ditch.
Their headstones line up like the chairbacks
of boys in the orphanage

of the Government Indian School.
In every scraggly row,
one tilts at a perilous angle.
Wet whips dangle

from the weeping willow.
They have entered the iron vault
of earth. Under a turned-up
barrow, they swallow her salt—

what in our mouths, too, will be,
with the flinty sparks of stars,
the taste of eternity
when the cortege of cars,

in a cloud of dust, withdraws,
and all is barrenness.
The wind its passage raised
is shaking in the haws.

II. A Hill Village
One of Los Hermanos de Sangre, the Brothers of Blood, Speaks.

Filling the grooves of his name,
a late spring snow
blots out the black pain
of Inocencio

from his marble stone,
swallowing all sound
where he lies within
the barbwired holy ground.

Good Friday. Viernes Santo.
The death of every bell.
Mirrors, being punished,
turn and face the wall.

'Mano! Remember Christmas?
Season of bells and meat!
And the basins ringing last night
for the washing of the feet.

The church doors left wide open
to the mild night air.
And the smiling dog who trotted
in to say her prayer.

Spiritus Sanctus
whispered the bells at Mass.
The snow, immaculate,
falls into the razor grass

where my brothers leave
pink stains beneath bare feet.
Confess! Confess! Confess!
hisses the freezing sleet.

The feminine wail of the flute
weeping over the scales.
The bass drum in my temples
that drives home the nails.

Snowflakes soft as ash
stirred by the wind around
the slow arc of the lash
float upward and descend

burning, now, to pour
into the sacred sign,
the three cuts near my spine
slit by the Picador.

He makes veronicas
with the gonfalon.
The white bull of the wind

grazes his bloodied hand.

The fraying nerves of the fife.
Cessation of every sound
for the Procession of Blood
in which the bells are drowned.

III. The Morada. La Muerte

Death stands straight in her cart.
Her nose is in the air,
although she has no nose.
She aims the poisoned dart
of her breath at us.
Her arrow-hand is swift.
Her knuckles, scabbed with bark,
will not relax their grip
until the arrow-tip
lies quivering in its mark.

Pray for a good death,
but what death is good?
Her eyes outstare our eyes.
Her kisses are wormwood.
We breathe her waxen breath.
Death's sunken bust endures
while we, who were so beau,
so cool, so free of care,
and young, my friend, qué no?—
approach her on all fours.

IV. El Santuario de Chimayó

Guillermo tells everyone
Guillermo sold the field
because the earth, no virgin,
got stinting in her yield.

And the only *huero*

he can tolerate
is the barley straw
beneath his horse's feet.

But Guillermo doesn't own a
horse so far this year.
"¡Qué lástima!" he sighs
into his Corona.

"The only *huero* I like
is the blond head on my beer."
"¡Cerveza!" he cries. "¡Cerveza!"
A cry cried from the heart.

A fair-haired man
sucks down his Coors,
afraid the holy service
is about to start.

The line for the taco stands
blends into the line for church
and the line for the PortaSans.
Pigeons coo from their perch.

Inside, perpetual dusk
becoming the dark night.
Once your eyes adjust,
everything's red or white.

A sword glints white. The Lord's
discarded robe is red.
A red baldric for the carpenter
who nails him to the boards.

Hanging from a tack,
spine arched against the splintery
timber, thick neck thrust
hard against the cross,

eyes open but rolled back,
a terrible Christ.
His upper, unforgiving
teeth look very sharp.

A bloodless Reconquest!
From the height of a cloudy alp,
San Rafael angles his coup stick
toward a dripping scalp.

To the right, above,
fluttering on a disc,
wings of a white dove,
a sprig of tamarisk.

Filing past the altar's
gaily painted rail,
teens in tanks and halters
hide out from the hail.

One couple stands apart.
He rubs her arms, bare.
Her hand strokes his cheek
and rests lightly there.

They have taken a vow of silence
until the *matraca* strikes three.
They have no need for words.
Anyone can see.

Watching how their hearts
smoke in a green cage,
I smell bees and blood.
I see my wife at that age.

I'd confess my sins,
I'd confess my lies,
just to be able to look
like that into her eyes.

We pass into the room
favored by the tours—
the testimonials
of miraculous cures.

Assorted canes and crutches
hang from the ceiling beams.

Two saints in fly-screened hutches
hear confessions and dream.

Sharp click of billiard balls
comes from the monks at their beads.
A forest of walking sticks
is climbing up the walls.

There's Santiago Matamoros
hung with purple hearts and keys,
dogtags, scapulars,
licenses, rosaries.

Saint "Death-to-the-Moors!" James
and his whole platoon
might be reactivated.
(There's an election soon.)

Next to three plaster San
Franciscos de Asís,
Mary cradles her son
across her ancient knees.

On the wall behind her,
(wearing their hats in church!)
snaps of two policemen
and one of their murderer.

Rosewater's splashed on her hands.
The window, opened a crack,
lets in a gust of onions
from the taco stands.

There's a picture of Guadalupe
—a mosaic, I mean—
made with cherry, menthol, and lemon
cough drops and black beans.

There's El Santo Niño
in a cockle hat; a shell,
scalloped, briny, gilded,
on his rich lapel.

Expectant mothers whisper
in the pink shell of his ear;
missing children leave him
their old shoes to wear.

Piercing the inner dark,
a burning fishhook trolls
its barbed question mark
where a bare bulb glares down

over women crying in Spanish,
over a white dish,
over San Rafael
with his string of gutted fish.

Hot wax fumes and drips
onto a tile beside
a china Magdalena,
real lipstick on her lips.

There's a xeroxed photo,
taken by his wife,
of a man who disappeared
in 1988,

last seen in Española
by the Duke City gate.
It's stapled to a brief
description of his clothes—

brown pants, brown shirt, brown shoes,
and his red tattoos—
JESÚS on his left arm,
on his right, a rose.

There's a photo of La Muerte
in her chariot,
beside a saint with raised
finger to his lips—

Juan Nepomuceno,
patron of confessors?

—or Judas Iscariot?
Hanging from a rafter,

a frayed slingshot? A truss?
King David, reminding
the way we are living
will be the death of us.

A sign for *El Pozito*
points to a low door.
You bow your head to enter.
There's a dirt hole in the floor.

Hung on the mud wall,
a bloody Sacred Heart
proclaims in needlepoint
"Jesús es Amor!"

Like Lourdes, only more humble.
Not holy water, but holy dirt.
Untidy, lovely jumble
in four rooms, like the heart.

As the vigil proceeds
through the days of Holy Week,
more pilgrims eat in the courtyards;
some fast; some are just broke;

one hugs a five-foot cross
and a two-foot coke;
one nods off to the candles
whose prayers go up in smoke;

clutching a plastic bag
full of healing dirt,
a boy, shouting "Fag!"
throws stones at a man in a skirt;

old rivalries are decided
with jagged bottle or blade,
the river's drunken bragging
not to be gainsaid.

The Santa Cruz River
with its bank of blackened grass
holds in its swirling current
the woodgrain of the cross.

Snow falls. The river grumbles
through these poor acres, farmed
with a prayer and a blade,
where even the olive is armed

and rank as the rose with thorns.
It's either drought or flood,
the road washed out for good.
Spring's when the mother ditch burns,

when a bent back sustains
every two-crow field,
and the Sangre de Cristo Mountains
redden under the rains.

Riding the wind overhead,
little bloody whips
of silk trouble the eye.
They fall at our feet. The red

catkins hemorrhage
into river water, black
as the road that leads to this place
on the soul's pilgrimage:

highway of wooden crosses,
highway of Mexican bars,
highway of ditch bosses,
highway of knife-wounds and stars.

GENE FRUMKIN

The Luminosity of Day

Photo: Cynthia Farah

"One of my primary efforts has been the attempt to express my responses to New Mexico. I came to Albuquerque in 1966 and experienced what can fairly be described as a culture shock. This was not so much due to the multiethnic population as it was because of the luminosity of day and the clear stars at night just a short distance from the city proper. Having been born in New York and raised in Los Angeles, I felt New Mexico was a vitally fresh encounter for me. I was awestruck by my natural surroundings as I had never been before."

A professor of English at the University of New Mexico, Gene Frumkin has influenced generations of aspiring poets in the Creative Writing Program. The author of eleven books, his most recent are *Saturn Is Mostly Weather* (Cinco Puntos Press, 1992) and *Comma in the Ear* (Living Batch Books, 1991).

In a book of poems called *Clouds and Red Earth*, published by Swallow Press Books in 1981, Frumkin explored his personal view of New Mexico. "It was mostly a record in some detail of my to's and fro's, my adaptation to this place, and also some of the glad and sad things that were happening to me."

"Stanford Street Poem," "White Panther," and "Salmon in the Pool" are three works that represent this process. The fourth poem printed here, "Saturn Is Mostly Weather," is also a composition of place, but in this case an evocation of the romance of Hawaii, where he spent two and a half years both as exchange professor and writer-in-residence.

His latest work focuses more on language itself "as object of a decentered subject. This doesn't mean," he says, "that I have abandoned place as a motivational source, but the place has changed to meditations on the Diaspora—as a Jew I wander into myself as in a sense a language terrain...."

WHITE PANTHER

I camped last night in the ravine
northeast of Taos where the white panther
was rumored several times in recent months.
During the night I was counseled twice,
once by footfalls outside the tent
and later by an Indian, tall and hatchet-nosed,
eyes brown and calm as a bear's.
He said, "Get up and look outside."

I opened the flap and there was the moon,
stony cold, slanting through my dream.
The spruce and pine were still.
The fire I'd built to cook my late meal
was a grey cloud of ashes.
I remembered the footfalls and thought,
"Of course, it was the white panther!
God has consented to believe in me."

When I awoke in the morning
a crow had gotten wedged into my chest.
His wings smashed about furiously
and his "caw-caw" was the voice
of the Indian laughing at me.
Despite his counsel I had slept through
my welcome. There is no white panther
northeast of Taos, not any more.

SALMON IN THE POOL

That was the earlier dream
in which I walked to the pool's edge
where one fish, a cloudy salmon,
tried to swim upstream. Of course
the pool's blue walls would not allow it.
I remembered saying, "There is

no stream." Later someone told me
the salmon was clearly
myself.
                    In the next dream
I was more reasonable. I stayed inside,
in my room, painting maps
on my walls in daring colors.
All of the maps resembled Africa
and I knew why even while I painted.
I wanted to go away, to become
my most ancient ancestors.
                                        Now
someone tells me I have gone
too far in locking my windows
against the light. I swim inside
myself. I draw charts for retirement
from all obligations, including
love. "You rationalize everything,"
she says. "You think
like a system."
                        Or a salmon, I think,
on its way across the Atlantic
to the great Red Sea. Yes,
I am repressed, as everyone is
who draws reason from movie-lot
walls. Even so, against death
and toward it, I tug
at the many shores where wisdom lives,
I pull the groaning water with me.

STANFORD STREET POEM

When living
                    even with people you love
boils you dry each day
                                        what music shall
calm you   Can the sky open *that* wide
to receive your cry
                        The gag of love

steals your tongue   what you know
of soil and sea   flowering and fall

As other bodies call to you
a woman's teeth a man's beard
you approach them   cold leaves in your legs
leaning on an old moonbeam
                                        the song:
a single crow on the naked bough

                snow on the Sandias now
                creamy fields below Taos

                water in hose will freeze

                nothing to reach for
you must
                dance

                        with the trees

SATURN IS MOSTLY WEATHER

Lying with her, watching the rain
pass through sunlight, I think about
the miles of love that lie
before me. Her eyes are closed
and she breathes in slow waves.
I can hear the rain washing off
the plumeria leaves, cleansing the tall
dirty palms.
                The distance ahead
must diminish, love by love,
and I delude myself in making a mask
of some god's face to see through.
We cannot share the mystery, she and I,
our dreams do not believe each other.

Her eyes circle around herself,
her sun, in the black starlit space
under her lids. Awake, I can't help
her going, I can only listen to wet wheels
passing over wet light outside the window.

She will say my name and again
it will be someone else's. All those loves,
little suburban planets apart and bound
to my death, orbiting far ahead
in some still undeveloped photographs.
Meanwhile, if I am not in bed
beside this woman, I must be elsewhere
not hearing the suddenly awakened silence,
which I realize is the rain's deliberate
cessation.   More harshly the sun
streaks across the opposite wall,
and the shadows are harsher. Morning is late,
I am older, I don't want to shave
or even wash my face in the glass.
I will send her away; she shows up
only as a shade in my eyes' dim
and mustardy gaze.   Then her mouth opens
just a whisper when her face
rolls slightly away from me, so I hear
our separation as the last evidence
of a moth's wavering into the dark.
The cycles continue, nothing ever ends
completely until the gutters themselves
crumble into fiery mutilated air.
Her fingers twitch on my thigh
as if they had come from another land.

GREG GLAZNER

Living in the Face of Death

Greg Glazner was born in Anson, Texas, and educated at Hardin-Simmons University and at the University of Montana.

"My poems often take as their starting points the landscape of the West—at times immense and impersonal, and at times a ground for conflicts between people. My sources are various: northern New Mexico, Texas farm life, suburban aspirations, television, Baptist oratory, the Montana wilderness."

From the Iron Chair, Glazner's collection of poems, was published in 1992 by W. W. Norton & Company. He is also the author of a chapbook, *Walking Two Landscapes* (State Street Press, 1984). His awards include the 1991 Walt Whitman Award from the Academy of American Poets and the Bess Hokin Award from *Poetry*. He teaches at the College of Santa Fe.

"I hope that, finally, my work is about themes: living in the face of death, of violence, of bitterness, and finding a way to praise that living without looking away from its real terms. And I hope that the music and emotional layerings of the poems are a central part of that praise."

Glazner resides near Tesuque.

FIN DE LA FIESTA

Los Conquistadores, Horseback, The Burning of Zozo-
bra, Streetdance, Sea of Trinkets, Coronation, Proces-
sion, Candlelight, Choir

At the duskfallen end of it, there were graces.
Downhill, the mock-adobe storefronts faded
and finally darkened, the glittering
misery of traffic eased a little,
and the torchbearer stooped at the switchback,
his lips tensed to hold his cigarette. He must have
paused to let the falseness leave him,
pressing the torchhead to a stack of pine,
his arm against the waist-high fire
shined with sweat, his eyelids gold.
There was a choir behind us, high-pitched
in their sentimental verses, but the surrender
in their voices, the amateurish earnestness
and the firelight on the path were undeniable.

In the dark we could hear the torchbearer
rasping as he climbed, slouching and lighting up
entirely, and shuffling on, half-silhouette again.
Then he was gone, and his luminarias
were set adrift in the lateness.
In the distance San Miguel, the mission
of the pueblo slaves, was muted to a black
relief in hotel lights, and music
from a bell choir somewhere floated
through the murmuring, the small, habitual bitternesses,
houses downhill lit before the news, the adlight rolling
like a sea-blue love of sleep across the fixtures.

But in the dark wash of the air, there were voices,
clerestory windows, the shadowy gathering of faces
stripped of everything but the need
to send up lights and sing. The towers
full of tolling at the end of mass, the street,
the first ranks of celebrants. It wasn't history
they entered, their candles, hundreds,
rippling toward us. It wasn't force
or crucifix or greed between the federal offices

and the trinket shops stripped down to their little
eyes of incandescence. Such a flickering progression
in the blankness. Faceless. The flames a current there.

At the atonal confluence where we waited, bell choir
and mariachis, whispers, *mas cerca mi bita*,
closer. Listen. He was gone, with his gold
eyes and his branch flame. Just the disembodied hands
and for their moments, bodies sidelit on the path
as if they passed through islands of original light.
There were graces. The young flashing through
the rich senselessness, so many ascensions,
cupped candles, palms flickering,
woodsmoke, breath. The vacuum.
Each face flushed brilliantly against it. Then not.

LEAVING THE VIGÍL STUDIO

under hung rugs and steel religious beads,
still stooped as if with their weight
onto the pavement, for once
to just let down, as visible heat
dissolves the eastfaced surfaces,
and shadows press a brief, whorled elegance
into an upturned palm,
a street's lineage of troweled earth
that promises to die entirely; for once
without false hope, without malice for its loss.

To let the high clouds darken us
on Water Street, cooling the benches sculpted
into the adobe walls, damping the slick glare down
in the storefront windows, as grimaces
slacken from the tourists' faces, and at our side
a salesman flexes all the rings and knuckles
of his grip, releasing the daughter's arm.

She leans against an archway ribbed
with blocks of crushed cinders, and snakes her hand

along the little fissures cracking upward
like a premonition from the pueblo mines,
easing three hundred miles out of mineshaft
nuclear caverns, into a shape she feels
unconsciously, staring into the poster shop.
Staring out, the owners see the dark scars
mortared off, driven back down under an atmosphere
of signs, loose pastel summer clothes, and the soft
pallor of shoppers, who even here
haven't purged the vacuum from their eyes,
sacks full of soap and beads;
who shuffle into the weakness of the afternoon,
its mute surfaces, its little omens.

L A R R Y   G O O D E L L

Photo: Diana Huntress

Native Is Old Hat

Larry Goodell was born in Roswell, New Mexico, in 1935 and got his B.A. degree from the University of Southern California. He moved to Placitas, New Mexico, in 1963 and founded Duende Press, which published new writing by Margaret Randall, Kenneth Irby, and Judson Crews, among others. His wife, Lenore, is a photographer and cartographer. Goodell has organized poetry readings in the Albuquerque area since 1970 and has developed his own "readings" into almost theatrical or performance events.

"I sing in speech given, when allowed, from my local point of view as a relatively nontraveling native New Mexican. My notebooks contain handwritten scores, I like to call them, rather than 'drafts,' since I don't really revise. I get an on-edgy joy while guiding a poem making itself up. The time of writing develops the subject of each poem and determines if there is any need for prop or mask to help perform it.

"Lenore and I have been gardeners throughout our twenty-five-year marriage, and again I come back to our three-quarter acre here twenty-five miles out of Albuquerque higher up where springs allow a good vegetable and flower garden and a lot to freeze late summer and every fall. It gets into my poems, these images."

Goodell's books of poetry include *Firecracker Soup*, poems 1980–1987 (Cinco Puntos Press, 1990) and *Out of Secrecy* (Yoo-Hoo Press, 1992). *The Mad New Mexican*, songs 1981–1986, is available on cassette tape. He received a National Endowment for the Arts Fellowship in 1983 and was recently the subject of a KNME-TV *Colores* program.

"Being a lifelong resident native has its problems. Grandma Goodell with

Dad and Aunt and Grandpa came from Kansas to New Mexico in a covered wagon, to Grenville back in the 1910s. So being native and having a love of a plural culture is old hat for me. Newcomers wax romantic about the state while I tend to see the poverty and ongoing problems. The sky and the space are renewed to us, though, especially when we return from a trip and everything seems large and clear."

THE HOUSE THAT MAKES IT SO
for the Creeleys

I drove by the old Creeley house
        because I wanted to write a poem.
There was the piano-shaped bedroom
        Bobbie had Von Shutze build.
The floors of adobe with sheep's blood sealer
        that kept crumbling in the old house,
The step-down new studio with that volcanic Jémez view
        where we sat & picked the energy of language apart
and I could put my life in art back together
        to go on in this isolated New Mexico way
where the others all seem taller, and *I*
        sit & improvise only sometimes to connect.
Their talking out the window of VW rebuilt engines
        or collaborations with Rauschenberg or Altoon,
The patio of corn & rhubarb & music to enchiladas
        Almaden white wine as
Back to the kitchen, the slow night weaved on
        and alternative worlds to where I was born
Played over the cassette player or hi-fi out to space
        and Max, or John, I never saw, or
Stan & Jane & Ed & Tuli & Jonathan & Ronald & Ann & George
        & on & on came through (I forgot Allen & Lawrence)
To meet like Gertrude Stein's patio in their adobe hacienda
        where children pulled apart & adults prospered
and friends analyzed until the dawn trailed off
        the always fresh love of poetry that was life, life blood.
If apprenticeship is anything, or hand to hand, a better poem
        commands itself to be written in the house that makes it so.

HUMAN NON-SEQUITUR

Humans don't know how to communicate with each other
Therefore I prefer figs, or pigs—figs have a built-in line through the trunk
    from one to one, as sensual treats flow through stems.
Pigs voice communication & wallow, intelligently, close to each other & fight
    with great discharge,
Which they have in common with humans, when they charge, & fight.
Fathers can't even talk with their sons: why should the sons always take the
    initiative.
Men can't even talk with each other, except in bars & hardly go *out of their
    way* to communicate.
Monkeys chatter & pick fleas off, & preen, everyone talks better to each
    other
Than humans, except possibly the women of the species, but they're only half.
So, alone, the human species male, wallows in his own pit of discovery.
His & *her* flesh is an unknown, a future enterprise where sexes are equal.
So doubly alone women turn to themselves having given up on men who are
    willing to talk.
There are always the dolphins, the cockatoos, the elephants, the apples &
    especially the cornstalks which rhyme with talk.
There's the mirror, for the lonely human. There's the sea talking to the air.
There are every which species managing communication, while the human
    egoistically, tries to carry on.

ALL OF LOVE

I can have all of love, played to a tired cello
Perked up to Bach's best, the message drums in the Congo
the cello, the Congo, the amazing Amazon, the woman
the River, the unpolluted Ocean, the nature harmonizers
the voices of the Globe in multivarious harmonies.
Two hundred & fifty years ago the music is still young
Buoyant to any mood, unaccompanied cello accompanied
in this life by this life—I mean, a flower in the atmosphere
one gives the other to imagination. Three moonflowers the other night
and the orchid cactus from the canopies of Guatemala
blooming one two three blooms on successive nights
in full burst of exotic white, sweetness and strange,
to wilt in the morning, we sleep in the only sleep there is side
by side by and in the aromatic air with rain, the late summer gone.

RENÉE GREGORIO

The Pulse under the Pulse

"Lately, I've been thinking about all the worlds we must move in and around and how very real each of those worlds is, and how, as poets, we work in ways that may appear peculiar to others. It is our business to pay attention to the strangest of details, to the pulse under the pulse, and to try to recognize the essential quality of an object or a dream-voice or an idea, and by doing so, to breathe new life into these things, to see in new ways."

Renée Gregorio's writing life took shape in England, where she completed her M.A. in creative writing at Antioch University and began publishing her poetry. One of the founding editors of the *Taos Review*, she is a former member of the jazz-poetry group Luminous Animal. Originally from the Boston area, she has been in New Mexico since 1985, six years in and around Taos and Lama and two years in Jacona, near Santa Fe. Currently, she works as a creative writing teacher and freelance editor. Renée is as obsessed with aikido as she is with poetry, and she is "in the business of following the heat and the light."

"I am struck with the idea of poetry as energy. And by the ways language can obstruct itself or stay out of the way of itself—by the ways the poem serves as vessel in some largely alchemical process using words, pens, pages, thoughts, sensations, images, blood, memory, and scent—mixing, till what emerges is something that can heal or transform. The point, for me, is to dig down into the stuff of my life, my particular surroundings (whether I'm at home by the cherry trees and acequia or traveling by train and waiting in the warm drafts of stations), and the particular voices of my dream-life.

"Though one can do this sort of diving anywhere, there is a way being in New Mexico supports such depth, such relationship to history and memory, such stillness. This is a good place to search for the still point within the many dances of what and who we are. It is a place where we are constantly reminded of the existence of rich, ancient cultures, and thus a place that advocates such a search within oneself. Here, the light supports us, the bloodred mountains support us, the sounds of drumming and singing support us, as well as the way we can actually have a relationship with the earth. Who would not be affected by such beauty—starkness and openness, and a sky so rich with stars?"

SILENT DIALOGUE

You want to be free of so many things,
yourself for one. And the heavy vigas.
You want to be free of the driving wind,
the empty canvas, the wilting strawberry plants.

I don't know how to walk here, among the ruins.
I trip on the rough-edged stones. It's too dry;
I want to water everything without asking.
The wind blows hard, delivering a whisper of *father*.

A silent, invisible yoke. You dream of morphine.
Another addiction, directing you to another sort of death.
But you say in the dream, *I have you and I don't want to die*.
Light against stone. The silence of a clenched muscle.

Some days I think I want to get married.
It's a matter of linguistics; I want to say *husband*.
By the Rio Chiquito, Catanya told me lobsters mate for life.
I thought of how many halves of couples I'd eaten.

I'm sorry; I was hungry. When we woke this morning,
we spoke without words of the wide, green field in the distance.
It was before the alarm went off, after the shrill of coyote.
Quick lightning split Pedernal.

It was more than the curve of your bent elbow, more
than the words we said that kept us together, more
than that particular intersection. We saw the fragile
leaf of the unflowering pansy and felt afraid.

A song is building inside the lining of our throats.

TWO FLOATING SHAPES

I am not in the shadow at my father's side.
I am of the noon, the long dark one that stretches
out from him directly. When he turns I am
never there because I am also turning.

I will keep turning towards the face of his absence.
It is a burning log I am watching till there's nothing
but ash and smoldering, the heat of it
drifting upwards.

When my father and I finally met,
I recognized the joining of two floating shapes,
the soldering of a deep rift.
I remember it as two shapes suddenly fitting.

I have been far out of body
in that odd place of tears,
the place that knows things
before they happen, the place
I have and am nothing.
I have felt the loss of the child,
the blood rushing out of me.
The loss of that father.

I am digging at the river of sleep.
I know the invisibility of roots
and how we want to grasp them anyway
in our bare hands. I have seen scars
on the trunks of aspens where people I don't know
carved the design of their initials.
The bark of those trees rose like skin does,
in that exact position of healing.

THE FINAL X

Leaving felt somewhat like suicide: the intentional
killing-off, stripping away the vestments of home.
Yet also like being born, the coming up
out of the dark into the light, the cry
at the sudden, sharp intake of breath.
If I had nowhere to go I also
had everywhere—the childless woman, bleeding.

Days worn threadbare with searching,
trying to find the sound my own name makes.
I learn to fall over someone
else's arms, crashing onto the mats,
X of bodies, peculiar and singular kind
of release I must have—protecting myself
from myself.

Desire is imagination's best offering.
A man calls at midnight on the full moon.
It's the old story: I want to know what's hidden
and the only way is *through and urgent*.
The voice at the far end of the telephone
wire spills. I hold it, hot and dark as my own blood.
Slowly, in the space that is both healing and nightmare,
I remember there's room for all the voices.

Wanting to be stronger and weaker than I am,
the branch in the wind, I spread myself thin
next to the trickle of water in the arroyo,
listen to the sound running down to the river.
I walk into this final settling on the other side
of desire, not expecting someone else
to be my vehicle for transformation. I live
in X's extremes. A stranger becomes
the sudden recipient of my truth—
hidden, numinous water table of grief,
river we swim in that is the same river.

J O Y   H A R J O

The Power of That Beautiful Image

"This place has everything to do with how I write. When I first began writing in the mid-1970s, I was slowly dying of the thing I thought I had escaped from in Oklahoma. It was the land that gave my life back to me, inspired me to write. Around that time I began learning a little of the Navajo language, and I became politically involved, which meant speaking out about who we are as Indian peoples, speaking out about the land."

Joy Harjo arrived in New Mexico in 1967, a high school student, a refugee from a difficult childhood. From a history of "destruction"... she has lived here "more than not" since then, and she always returns to this place where she knows she has "followed the destiny of her aunt, Lois Harjo, who first came here in the early 1900s, met Maria Martinez and her family at San Ildefonso Pueblo, and especially loved Taos Pueblo. Aunt Lois was a painter and also loved the light." Says Harjo, "She returns with me to this place, and I am aware of carrying her within. I owe my growing up to this place of amazing light, particularly Santa Fe and Albuquerque."

Born in Tulsa, Oklahoma, in 1951, a member of the Creek tribe, Harjo graduated from the Institute of American Indian Arts in 1968 and the University of New Mexico in 1976. She received her M.F.A. from the Iowa Writers' Workshop and completed the filmmaking program at the Anthropology Film Center. Her books of poetry include *She Had Some Horses* (Thunder's Mouth Press, 1983), the award-winning *In Mad Love and War* (University Press of New England, 1990), and, in collaboration with photographer/astronomer Stephen Strom, *Secrets from the Center of the World* (University of Arizona Press, 1989). She is currently a professor in the Creative Writing Program at the University of New Mexico.

She is working on an original screenplay, *When We Used to Be Humans*, for the American Film Foundation. Forthcoming is a children's book, *The Goodluck Cat* (Harcourt Brace Jovanovich), two books from W. W. Norton & Company, and an anthology of native women's writing, *Reinventing the Enemy's Language* (University of Arizona Press). She gives poetry readings nationally and internationally and plays saxophone with her band, Poetic Justice.

"One time when I was secretly fighting to stay alive I carried around a photograph of those scarlet cliffs that define Jémez country, the way they look when the sun first hits them as you drive west. I would pull that out anytime I thought I was losing the fight, and kept going. The power of that beautiful image worked, and this land continues to shimmer and speak to the root of my rebellious soul."

Harjo's many distinguished awards include the Josephine Miles Award from PEN Oakland, the William Carlos Williams Award from the Poetry Society of America, the Delmore Schwartz Award from New York University, the American Book Award, the Poetry Award from the Mountains and Plains Booksellers Association, and the 1990 American Indian Distinguished Achievement Award. She is the recipient of an Arizona Commission on the Arts Creative Writing Fellowship and two National Endowment for the Arts creative writing fellowships.

PROMISE

The guardians of dusk blow fire from the Rincons as clouds confer
over the Catalinas in the fading tracks of humans. I interpret the
blur of red as female rain tomorrow, or the child born with the
blessings of animals who will always protect her.

I am always amazed at the skill of rainclouds who outline the weave
of human density. Crickets memorize the chance event with rain-
songs they have practiced for centuries. I am recreated by that lan-
guage. Their predictions are always true. And as beautiful as saguaro
flowers drinking rain.

I see the moon as I have never seen the moon, a half-shell, just large
enough for a cradleboard and the child who takes part in the dance

of evolution as seen in the procession of tadpoles to humans painting the walls with wishes.

From the moon we all look the same.

In two days the girl will be born and nothing will ever look the same. I knew the monsoon clouds were talking about it as they softened the speed of light.

Cedar smoke in a prayer house constructed in the last century pervades my memory. Prayer lingers in the ancestral chain.

You can manipulate words to turn departure into aperture, but you cannot figure the velocity of love and how it enters every equation. It's related to the calculation of the speed of light, and how light prevails.

And then the evening star nods her head, nearby a lone jet ascending. I understand how light prevails. And when she was born it rained. Everything came true the way it was promised.

THE MYTH OF BLACKBIRDS

The hours we counted precious were blackbirds in the density of Washington. Taxis toured the labyrinth with passengers of mist as the myth of ancient love took the shape of two figures carrying the dawn tenderly on their shoulders to the shores of the Potomac.

We fled the drama of lit marble in the capitol for a refuge held up by sweet, everlasting earth. The man from Ghana who wheeled our bags was lonesome for his homeland, but commerce made it necessary to carry someone else's burdens. The stars told me how to find us in this disorder of systems.

Washington did not ever sleep that night in the sequence of eternal nights. There were whirring calculators, computers stealing names, while spirits of the disappeared drank coffee at an all-night cafe in this city of disturbed relativity.

Justice is a story by heart in the beloved country where imagination weeps. The sacred mountains only appear to be asleep. When we finally found the room in the hall of mirrors and shut the door I could no longer bear the beauty of scarlet licked with yellow on the wings of blackbirds.

This is the world in which we undressed together. Within it white deer intersect with the wisdom of the hunter of grace. Horses wheel toward the morning star. Memory was always more than paper and cannot be broken by violent history or stolen by thieves of childhood. We cannot be separated in the loop of mystery between blackbirds and the memory of blackbirds.

And in the predawn when we had slept for centuries in a drenching sweet rain you touched me and the springs of clear water beneath my skin were new knowledge. And I loved you in this city of death.

Through the darkness in the sheer rise of clipped green grass and asphalt our ancestors appear together at the shoreline of the Potomac in their moccasins and pressed suits of discreet armor. They go to the water from the cars of smokey trains, or dismount from horses dusty with fatigue.

See the children who became our grandparents, the old women whose bones fertilized the corn. They form us in our sleep of exhaustion as we make our way through this world of skewed justice, of songs without singers.

I embrace these spirits of relatives who always return to the place of beauty, whatever the outcome in the spiral of power. And I particularly admire the tender construction of your spine which in the gentle dawning is a ladder between the deep in which stars are perfectly stars, and the heavens where we converse with eagles.

And I am thankful to the brutal city for the space which outlines your limber beauty. To the man from Ghana who also loves the poetry of the stars. To the ancestors who do not forget us in the concrete and paper illusion. To the blackbirds who are exactly blackbirds. And to you sweetheart as we make our incredible journey.

THE PLACE THE MUSICIAN BECAME A BEAR
for Jim Pepper

I think of the lush stillness of the end of a world, sung into place by singers and the rattle of turtles in the dark morning.

When embers from the sacred middle are climbing out the other side of stars.

When the moon has stompdanced with us from one horizon to the next, such a soft awakening.

Our souls imitate lights in the Milky Way. We've always known where to go to become ourselves again in the human comedy.

It's the how that baffles. A saxophone can complicate things.

You knew this, as do all musicians when the walk becomes a necessary dance to fuel the fool heart.

Or the single complicated human becomes a wave of humanness and forgets to be ashamed of making the wrong step.

I'm talking about an early morning in Brooklyn, the streets the color of ashes, do you see the connection?

It's not as if the stars forsake us. We forget about them. Or remake the pattern in a field of white crystal or of some other tricky fate.

We never mistook ourselves for anything but human.

The wings of the Milky Way lead back to the singers. And there's the saxophone again.

It's about rearranging the song to include the subway hiss under your feet in Brooklyn.

And the laugh of a Bear who thought he was a human.

As he plays that tune again, the one about the wobble of the earth spinning so damned hard it hurts.

GERALD HAUSMAN

Photo: Hannah Hausman

Sharing across the Years

"I first came to northern New Mexico in 1965. At Highlands University Richard O'Connell suggested I try my hand at translating Navajo material. I came through the anthropological backdoor of Navajo studies, trying, in a sense, to translate a culture I did not really understand. And here I am now, nearly thirty years later, working at the same material."

Gerald Hausman holds a B.A. in English Literature from New Mexico Highlands University in Las Vegas. He has worked as a wrangler on a dude ranch, house painter, adobe slinger, trade book editor, creative writing teacher, poet-in-residence, and storyteller.

"Writing became, quite by accident, a by-product of experiential life with Indian people; and I became, also accidentally, a cultural by-product myself. The writing is only valid if it does honor to the people who shared their hearts with me. For this reason, I write very slowly and carefully. My work is a communal sharing of lore. This sharing goes back and forth across the years. We learn, that is all."

Hausman's numerous books include *Turtle Island Alphabet: A Lexicon of Native American Symbols and Culture* (St. Martin's Press, 1993), *The Gift of the Gila Monster: Navajo Ceremonial Tales* (Touchstone Books/Simon and Schuster, 1993), and *Tunkashila: From the Birth of Turtle Island to the Blood of Wounded Knee* (St. Martin's Press, 1993). His book for children, *Coyote Walks on Two Legs*, is forthcoming from Philomel/The Putnam Publishing Group in 1995.

He lives in Tesuque, New Mexico, with his wife and two children.

JUNIPER

The way the bark looks, wind-peeled and gnarled
Like a woman
Wetted in the rain.
Saw the wood in hot summer, throw it in the chunk
Pile for the cold winter to come. The red, dead
Juniper dust carries the pungent scent of
Red chili; sweet dust reminds us as it floats into
The face: San Ildefonso Pueblo.
Warm in woolen blankets, winter bells of dancers
And the chili by firelight after.
Water juniper—she drinks just once in a while—
The loving wood
That warms us: once, when we cut
Twice, when we burn
Three times
When we smell the smoke and remember summer in the
Sweet grain.

THE OLD WAYS

He was old enough to know better; the young spunk
Mare he was riding slid on the slick cobble,
And, falling, crushed the old man's legs.
Nurses roped him to his bed, that old Santo Domingo man
Who wouldn't be operated on. They tied him in,
Lashed him to the bedpost in the hospital prison ward
Where he thrashed himself free in the night
And made good his escape, fleeing with his grandson.
This day as the sun burns and the year turns,
He tells his grandson: "The old ways are our ways,
And they will never die."

JUDYTH HILL

Photo: Murrae Haynes

Poetry for the Future Human

"I chose New Mexico. Chose her above all others for beauty, for the possibility of preserving still-pristine landscape, air and waters, for her swirl of tangy cultures, and green chile and melted cheese on everything....I like to yell and fly. And, oh, God, I love to write so much. I love the balancing of craft and passion, the work behind the work. I get hot and flushed and sweaty—it's the best. And then, I love to read it to you. Because that's what completes the circle of the creative act: it's not 'whole and sole' without your presence."

Judyth Hill is a full-time writer, performer, and teacher of poetry. She moved to Santa Fe twenty years ago from a New York City childhood and Sarah Lawrence education that included studying with Galway Kinnell and Cynthia MacDonald. She has a son and a daughter. She had a marriage, a bakery, two movie theaters, several dogs, and many cats. She never stopped writing.

She has been teaching an on-going women's writing class for five years; works as New Mexico artist-in-residence, a job that includes residencies at the New Mexico Boys' School in Springer and on the Navajo Reservation in the Four Corners area. Judyth also teaches in Very Special Arts, the AIDS Writing Program, and the Artists in the Parks Summer Program. The author of three chapbooks, her fourth collection of poetry, *Men Need Space*, is forthcoming from Stony Mesa Publications in Santa Fe. Her column, "Foodbeat," for the *Albuquerque Journal North* is in its fifth year.

"I am dedicated to studying and teaching the creative process as the next major phase in the development of the Future Human—all the while living seriously rural, on a wild mountain, in a handmade post-and-beam home in the Strike valleys between Las Vegas and Mora. It's a life about passion, and choices. And having fun. Admiring the plain, astonishing beauty everywhere present, and not losing sight of the fallen in Somalia, Bosnia, and the AIDS epidemic.

"Making love, dinner, and connections. Getting the point, listening deeply to the music of the ordinary, the wisdom of elders, infants, and others, and the night wind moving through ponderosa pines from my front porch. And singing it back, as best my innate talents and acquired skills will grant me."

GRIST FOR GRACE

Let me speak for the gray-green lichen,
Know how the Blackjacks go crone in harsh weather,
or on account of mistletoe.
Help me say how winter comes in on a red-gold downbeat,
an orchestra of oak.

Sing me a forest.
Sing me in the sweet pitch of ochre, the bassy rusts.
Play me in the key of mountains,
Rising always above myself.
Hum the rustling needles of the pine's constant undressing.
Make me naked to any season.

Make me open to the tender rays of late sun.
Call my name in the sounds of absent water.
Write my address this way:
Turn right at the quartzite boulder,
Go straight 'til you remember your first kiss
and the smell of toast that first morning.

Dress me in evergreen, in blue spruce and fir.
Make an altar of the ordinary.
Piñon cones and the feathers of Steller's jays.
Write me a simple story, hummingbird's soar,
raven's wing and rock bed.

Tickle me with Turkey feathers.
Make me laugh.
How many religions does it take to screw in a light bulb?
Dance me along a sacred maze, back into my body,
That other, most hallowed ground.

SAMURAI ANGELS

I heard your name in my dream last night.
It was your childhood name and I was calling you.
There was an angel on every stair.
There was light from four directions.

It was your childhood name and I was calling you.
Tell me eleven names for wind, I said.
There was light from four directions.
Tell me how you followed the scent of daffodils through
          the streets of London.

Tell me eleven names for wind, I said.
I'm one thought away.
Tell me how you found a square filled with flowers in a
          dark city.
The angels are calling our names out loud.

I'm one landscape away.
Any moment could be Japan.
The angels are calling our names out loud.
Their wings are light and cherry blossom, we could hear
          temple bells ringing on any street.

Any landscape could be Japan.
You were born there.
There will always be plum blossom, can't you hear the
          silence in the temples around us?
I can write you three lines and there will be cranes in
          all of them.

You were born there.
After love we breathe in Japanese, our sleeping bodies
            form the character for light.
I can write you three lines and there will be the way you
            loved your father in all of them.
There's a secret in Haiku: I'll tell you.

After love we breathe in Japanese, our sleeping bodies
            form the character for angel.
After love the taste of saki is silky and fierce.
There's a secret, I'll tell you:
Haiku is really four lines, but the last line is silent.

After love the taste of saki is silky and fierce.
See how gently I write us into your past.
The fourth line in Haiku is a temple.
I call your secret name for the last time.

See how delicately I write us into your past.
Under Fujiyama, I know you are weeping.
I call your childhood name for the last time.
I hold you. Your tears rhyme with the grain of light
            woods,
The sound of taps for your father.

(A DREAM OF FRIDA)

Vines grow up, around the coverlet
where the artist sleeps.
A ghost of hyacinths floats above her
wired to explode into a destiny of calamity.

She dreams herself into her future, where vines grow
around a wisteria trellis and she's walking,
walking the Hacienda's veranda, and vine's entwine
flower to needle, leaf to bud, to bloom, seed
and leaves again, then dry, they fall,
fall and blow.

Easterly wind, October's heat takes the bosque down into golden,
vines grow up, around a skeleton month
where no mother calls the name of her daughter,
no one strokes her head, calls her, mi corazon, mi caratida.

She's alone by the Rio, a glint of light
shiny coins of water music clinking,
moving swift over rocks, where vines grow up
in the sleep of Aspens.
They quiet, calm them, as horses do, by breath.
A tree breathes into Autumn:
A woman sleeps under a yellow quilt of leaves.

Grasses lay down, apples are sudden
in an orchard of over.

November calls her by name.
Something she can't see, strokes her again.
Her mother becomes visible on the stairs of the Hacienda.
Her mother is singing on the veranda,
a girlhood song in perfect Castilian.
No tiene miedo, she sings.
She sings of shadow and light, sombre y luce.
She strokes the bannister as she descends.
She walks the long road to the river,
the cottonwoods arch overhead.
Moonlight peers through bare branches and clouds.

She sees color. The night is a new dress.
She carries a bouquet of bones to the edge of the water.
Vines grow up around the fallen poplars,
she never catches her breath.
She runs from the voice calling her name.
The road is stuttering in tree.
The trees sing in Spanish of falling.

The yellow quilt is spread under a wisteria vine
in full fragrant bloom.
Her hair is tied back with a lilac ribbon.
Her mother wears a dress of shadow.
She is drowning in her bed of white bones.

She hasn't worn lace in years.
Her day is set to go off on a hairpin trigger.

Anything can make her go down that road.
She saw it once, quickly around a corner in the Museum.
She's walking, walking up the stairs dressed in fallen leaves.
It was a landscape painted in 1806.
It was the French countryside, but exactly the same.
That gold, the bones, the leaves in drift.

She never knew the painter's name.
She called it once in a dream.
He came to her dressed in velvet.
He lay in the dark bed, whispering
Sombre, sombre, te amo.
She whispered back.

There was no map to this place.
The Museum was in Milan.
The dream was tangled in her hair.
The vines grew up the trellis to the second floor.
She slept on as if nothing had happened.

ELIZABETH
SEARLE LAMB

True Moments

Elizabeth Searle Lamb was born in 1917 in Topeka, Kansas, and grew up surrounded by books and music. She studied the harp beginning at an early age and attended the University of Kansas (B.A. and B.M.), where she met her future husband, writer Bruce Lamb. They were married in 1941 in Trinidad. While Bruce was in the Amazon procuring wild rubber from the jungle for the war effort, Elizabeth lived as the only English-speaking person in the small Brazilian town of Santarem. With no harp, the typewriter became increasingly important creatively, and she began to write.

Bruce's career as a tropical forester took Elizabeth and their daughter, Carolyn, to Honduras, Puerto Rico, Panama, Colombia, and eventually New York City. In 1977, they moved into an old adobe house beside an acequia on Acequia Madre in Santa Fe. Since Bruce's death in 1992, Elizabeth has been involved in handling his literary properties as well as her own writing.

"I've always loved words; I learned to read before I went to kindergarten. Much of my writing is sparked by place and personal, often new, experience. Almost all my haiku are true moments from my life, a way of capturing the kernel of a fleeting awareness."

Lamb is the author of numerous books of haiku, including *Casting into a Cloud: Southwest Haiku* (From Here Press, 1985). Her work has been widely anthologized, and has appeared in Canada, Japan, Romania, Poland, England, Australia, and China as well as in the United States. She is the editor of the Haiku Society of America's *Frogpond* magazine.

"On my first trip to New Mexico the phrase 'the sky-starred Babe' began to haunt me—from where I knew not—until we drove to the ruins of San

Gregorio de Abo. There, suddenly, was the poem "Mission Ruins," virtually intact. New Mexico continues to be a powerful stimulus as I remain open to its landscape, its people, and its cultures."

----

almost daybreak
          only once
that cry of the raven

on the ditch bank
a scattering of wild plums
purple shadows

a white horse
drinks from the acequia
          blossoming locust

raised by a hoist
and spring songs of little birds
   Cristo Rey's re-cast bells

this morning
          the rooster too
from far away

the broken harp string
curving
into sunlight

he prunes the juniper
bright blue berries falling
beneath the wind chimes

the brown-robed priest
focusing on Indian dancers
sunflash off his Leica

autumn's full moon
on the far side of the church
the blackest shadows

Española lowriders
circle the sunwashed plaza
again and again

half silted under
            the dead puppy
after spring run-off

    far back under a ledge
the ancient petroglyph   faint
    water sound

        tossing a stone
        down an abandoned mine shaft—
        the setting sun

        a lizard inching
        with the shadow of the stone
        nearer the cave's mouth

        a flight of birds
        breaks the stillness of sky
        no cloud moves

        a candle burns
        to the Virgin of Guadalupe
        —scent of roses

        field of wild iris—
        the pinto pony
        kicks up his heels

        wind in the sagebrush—
            the same dusty color
                    the smell of it

            a blue pickup
            rattles over the cattle guard
            dust devils

windswept mesa
the Navajo ghost hogan crossed
by ravenshadow

early blizzard
the faintest cries of wild geese
in the dark, in the snow

MISSION RUINS
San Gregorio de Abo

How the wind keens through the staring window holes
and vacant doorways leading from nothing into nothing;
how the one great standing wall of rough red rock looms
menacing and desolate against the darkening sky;
how this unwalled space where Franciscan Brothers walked
is filled with a kind of presence, a kind of whispering...

we went out from here to stalk the sky-starred Babe
whose birth was Holy Mystery to us, learning
in those rough paths of the pueblos—leather
of our sandals growing thin as trembling aspen leaf—
what was the radiance in the meaning of Love

we studied from all the Holy Texts, eyes aching
in the smoky, guttering light of candles,
seeking for some essence of the penetrating Wisdom
of that precocious Twelve-year-old confounding
all the prophets in their ancient Temple

our robes, much patched, grew stained and dusty—
the water in the deep arroyo being scarce—
as we sought for all the meanings
of the tree-hung Man who died upon a Cross

so we worked and walked, chanted at dawn and dusk
our prayers and plainsongs in the Sanctuary,
yet we knew, only death knowing death,
that not until Apache's arrow found the breast
would knowledge come to the marrow of the bones

and to some of us at the end, perhaps
there came some vision of that Light ...
and to some of us, perhaps, at the end
there came some echo of that Voice ...

How the wind keens through these unceilinged halls
and all the words are solitary stars snuffed out
by one swiftly scudding cloud. Listen ... far
across the piñoned mesa a coyote throws back his head
and howls, howls to greet the rising of the moon.

DONALD LEVERING

Continuing to Arrive

"The arrival in New Mexico continues with every piñon picking season, with every solitary hike down arroyos, arroyos that may open on broad streambeds or narrow to pictographic canyons, or shrink to labyrinthine passageways where prairie rattlers await your passing heat as a rabbit's. The cloying chamisa, the scent of crushed sage, the chile *ristras* adorning doorways, the relentless gritty spring winds, the cool high pines, the surreal lava beds of the Malpais, all keep arriving even as they've been here always."

Donald Levering's work has appeared in over one hundred literary journals. He has worked as a groundskeeper, teacher on the Navajo Reservation, freelance journalist, and management analyst; and now, in Santa Fe, he is director of the statewide Child Support Enforcement Division's computer system. He was a National Endowment for the Arts Fellow in 1984 and is winner of the University of California at Irvine's five thousand dollar Quest for Peace Writing Contest. At Bowling Green State University, where Levering received his M.F.A. in Creative Writing, he was a Devine Memorial Fellow in Poetry.

"I begin before I begin, when memories, reading, dreams, words begin their yeasty growth, a growth of days or weeks. And then I begin again as the day does, the blank screen gradually filling with words as dawn dims the stars. It's a rule that those which come quick and clean remain mostly as they first came, and those that come through dint and craft require more birthing. Later, I begin again, relentless and merciless editor, cutting, replacing, moving, sometimes beginning again, never looking back or saying from where it came."

WEAVING CAVE—FRIJOLES CANYON
for Camas

The ladder of lashed branches
is a letter
from the lost Anasazi language
It leads to the vowel
of a cave
hollowed out of the mesa wall
by rainwater

The wind blows across the mouth
the first notes
of the weavers' song

A cool round room
that could have been used
for birthing
before the looms
were lifted up the ladder

and the forked limbs
were secured to the ceiling
for the framework
of old stories

And holes were dug for the feet
of the looms
before knees and buttocks wore
blue stone into dust

A crow's view
of the pueblo below
where the sun was daily ground
into cornmeal

While the blankets rose on their frames
like ochre fires
for the season of sleet and long stories
for the time of withdrawing of ladders
the room suddenly silent
not even the clacking of looms

Photo: Marsha Littlebird

A Ceremonial Participation

Harold Littlebird is a Native American of Pueblo ancestry from Laguna and Santo Domingo pueblos. He lived in California and Utah for most of his childhood, returning to New Mexico as a teenager. At that time in his life, he was first introduced to village ceremony and began to learn more about his ancestry through religious practice. In particular, he began to listen to stories about the creation that had been passed down through the generations.

"The value of the stories became focused and real as I began to observe in a different way the 'writings' within my Pueblo landscape. Geographic sites of ancient rock drawings and petroglyphs, along with religious shrines and numerous abandoned ruins, the ancestral homes of my forefathers, added meaning and visual definition to that tribal history I was just beginning to sense."

Harold Littlebird has received many awards, including a National Endowment for the Arts Crafts Fellowship for pottery. A multidisciplinary artist with a national reputation as poet, potter, songwriter, and performer, he has been an artist-in-residence in schools throughout the United States, including a recent residency in Alaska. He has recorded two cassettes of his poetry and music, *A Circle Begins* and *The Road Back In*. His book of poetry *On Mountains' Breath* (Tooth of Time Books, 1982) is in its third printing.

"As I actively write poetry, compose songs, and joyfully celebrate daily life, it becomes increasingly clear that the physical and spiritual landscape of my homeland, the Southwest, helps me obtain creativity. For this gift from the Creator, I am truly thankful."

In a child's memory
kerosene lanterns faintly glow
clean water & alfalfa offerings
in freshly swept corrals
welcome their arrival

Summer's flowered shawl fades, retreats
wrinkled in Autumn's icy howl
first snow dusts Mt. Taylor's distant peaks
seemingly edible layer of purple popcorn clouds
swim the frigid, evening sky
as October gloomily departs
but, I remember, it is always much like this
Somehow
just before they come
bringing our loving relations, long departed

Grandfathers & Grandmothers, Mothers & Fathers
Aunts, Uncles, Brothers & Sisters
all our loved-ones, returning
re-united
feasting with the living

Hear now, the wagon wheels groan
and their tired horses' hooves plod
familiar dirt roads

On the earthen floor, prayerfully
prepared food is placed
steaming pottery bowls of red & green chile
with chunks of soft, mushy potatoes in savory broth
racks of greasy, roasted mutton ribs
piles of fresh tortillas, & sliced loaves of oven-baked bread
cups of dark, creamed coffee
sweetened, in remembrance
with heaping spoons of white crystal sugar
fresh, golden corn-on-the-cob, salt & peppered
and glasses of cool, refreshing water

All their favorite foods
peeled, squishy bananas
for Granpa, because he had no teeth

or baked apples, soft, shriveled & cut
slippery, oily sardines with thin, pungent slices of onion
stewed prune pies with flakey, Crisco crusts
tangy fruit sections nestled in porcelain bowls

And for you, Mom, a special soft salmon salad
mashed & boned, mixed with creamy mayonnaise
crisp celery chunks, chopped onion & strong, crushed garlic
just the way you liked it
and the way Marsha and I remember

vapors sweet, spiced & scented
fill our waiting home

We open the doors, and quietly, pray

      "Come in, sit down, eat
      We've been waiting...
      Welcome, all of you
      Eat lots
      You make us happy that you have come!"

JANUARY 30TH, 1989
Albuquerque, NM

Misting dusk crowned purple
Under amber light of Central & Yale

Above the slushing, coughing traffic
Rain-washed walls of Campus Pharmacy
Echo cacophonous chorus of crow

Non-synchronous caw-caw callings
Weigh these teary skies

Spellbound, I stand, neck craned upward
To crow flushed firmament

As ebony wings flash
In & out of the eyes' deception

Flit into nothingness

Return, charred snow flurries
Flapping, darting
Pound this darkened Winter's eve

Enmasse
To slender treetops they precariously cling
Blown back & forth in cooling night breath

Sleek, noisy silhouettes by thousands
Grace the sleeted streets
Caw-cawing deep folds of weathered night

Fasten to twisting tree
Beaks cocked & singing
Ruffed feathers swirl magic
Pulse to another attention

Winged brothers hold me in trance
Fine-tuned to new dance
Raise a bright song

On joyous sky streams
Raspy, branch top symphony
Electrifies the night-glow purple
To who would listen without ears
Awaking the child from stagnant sleep

Words have little meaning tonight
For feather music heals the heart
Lifts caring beyond silkened flight
On angelic, purposeful wing

FEAST DAY PREPARATION

There's a heaven-like pocket
Absent

Two, doe-eyed girls
Young & sassy
Lived here once
The man they knew as father, a child himself
Fled parenthood
Left them abandoned, unattended

Lethargic, that same man, a father, twice more
Holds that lost happiness at arm's length
Scared to embrace that harsh memory

Instead, transfers that pain
To his back
Becomes warped & hunched
Limbs stiff & cramped like an arthritic old man

Once he was a dancer
Lithe, strong with relocated dreams
Displaced dreams of home

He's seen that visionary bathhouse before
But where?
Heard that river rumbling, deep

The boy-father
Frightened
Clutches that fear
Like he clutches his back
And winces

Yet, beyond his pain lies hope
Like damp passage beneath rivers
Or beacon fires on desert floor
Calling the pilgrimed thousands

Those ruins once more seek
Search the memory sand
Turn the heaping ash pile under
Where deciphered meanings lie
Hidden between light & shadow

Trace this resolute day into night
How the wind plays this neglected canyon

Like the echoed mind of non-sleep
Alpha tranced

Glimpsed from the ether
Clues hold crystal truths
Break chains
Free the encumbered soul

Emotion transposed
I bear the nightmarish response
I am responsible
Realize, as twisted bones crack
The hidden, pinched nerve lie

Breath squares the dawning sun
Gemini faintly glimmers
The waxing moon, lucid shadow in repose
I awaken feverish, but placid
Remember my cloudy past
Begin the rough ride through it

Fight to remain focused for Self
And these children
Teetering that sublight residuum of dream

Reach that elusory cup, half-full
Drink lustrately
Knowing I am alive
I   AM   ALIVE!

This pain reminds —

FEBRUARY 3RD, AN EXCERPT

From dream deep slumber
I sleepily arise

Watch the North sky crack
Open her luminous 'back door'
Let my father slip through
Where he travels like shimmery light

In essence, I could have followed
But no!
That dance is not yet mine
I've much to learn, remember

Faraway miles separate me
From your final earth bed
Here, sorrow tears run freely
But, I'm near your glowing astral plain

Spirit never dies!

Travel in peace, *Oou-shra-dhu-ah*

I'm grateful for the life you gave me
Grateful for communion of parental love
Creating me, your last earth son

I saw you departing frail dwellings
That housed your soul
Flesh gives way to spirit, but
Spirit never dies!

Your Great-Granddaughter, Micaela Nicole
Will have your loving star gaze
Long into continuum
Searching vibrant traditions
Heavenly blessed

Travel on father
To higher places of unending, rippling light
Know your grandchildren honor you
And the people remember, *Oou-shra-dhu-ah*
The brilliance of sunshine
That sacred place where light first strikes

J O A N   L O G G H E

**New Mexico Writer with a
Pittsburgh Heart**

Photo: Julie Bennet

"I've been in New Mexico twenty years, and there is no place else I can imagine living. Not that I'm content here. I used to mourn for the ocean. Now I pine for cities. To walk down the block and buy orange juice seems exotic and luxurious. I have lived a rural life all these years, gardening, bearing children, and staying married; but it's the city girl who sings the poems."

Joan Logghe has lived in rural northern New Mexico, forging a style that blends her eastern, urban Jewish roots with the daily realities of raising three children outside of Española in a house she and her husband, Michael, built themselves. Themes of domesticity, marriage, ethnicity, family memory and history, and escape fantasy come together in her work to make a decidedly female voice that is wry, poignant, evocative, and at times, sharp with the recognition of truth.

In 1991, she received a National Endowment for the Arts fellowship in poetry, the only one awarded to a New Mexico writer that year. A longtime artist-in-residence in the state's schools, prisons, and nursing homes, Joan also works as poetry editor of *Mothering* Magazine. Her publications include three chapbooks: *Poems from the Russian Room* (Superstition Press, 1989), *A Lunch Date with Beauty* (FishDrum, 1990), and *What Makes a Woman Beautiful* (The Pennywhistle Press, 1993).

"My writing process has been much the same since I was a teenager. When the urge to write occurs, I need paper and pen now. It's like a craving for chocolate—I gotta have it. I've written poems on junk mail in my friend's car at Heron Lake, at night when it was too dark to see my words. I've written during the groups I teach, which is a different kind of luck. Sometimes I type at my desk, which is usually piled as high as the machine.

"I can write in the midst of family because I have very strong concentration for very brief amounts of time. I write poems, not novels, so the life and art fit. One Sunday, I wrote the final poem for a series called *The Sophia Poems*. I had been writing them over a period of ten years and realized that this lovely persona, Sophia, was left living alone with her dog in the mountains. She had to die; that was the proper end for her saga. As I began typing, my small daughter, Hope, arrived, and I said, 'Give me five minutes, I'm writing.' She set the timer on the stove, and I wrote the poem. Sophia indeed died as she had lived, with eccentric grace. I felt relieved and said, 'I'm back.' My family told me I had thirty seconds to spare.

"I value life as much as art. It has been my task to balance my two great loves. I succeed, and I fail. New Mexico is behind me like a movie backdrop I ride my horse in front of. I love the scenery but don't know what is real—the life, the landscape, or the poems. I know my children and husband are real; they don't let me forget."

HIGH SCHOOL GRADUATION PANTOUM

The dark boy leans against his pickup truck.
His heart widened into Romeo since he met my daughter.
I say to myself, "It's not worth creating a tragedy."
With the Blood Mountains behind them for Verona.

His heart widened into Romeo since he met my daughter,
a girl pulling him by the arms down the driveway
with the Blood Mountains behind them for Verona,
the wild plum blooming, they will make sour fruit.

A girl pulling him by the arms down the driveway,
not long ago, her arms reached, her face ached red for me.
The wild plum blooming, it will make sour fruit.
Passions so sweet, grape couldn't turn wine without it.

Not long ago her arms reached, her face ached red for me,
crying through play-pen bars as I gardened,
passion so sweet, grape couldn't turn wine without it.
I thinned lettuce, her stomach full of milk and need.

Crying through play-pen bars as I garden.
Time is a rascal magpie pecking at the corn.

I thinned lettuce, her stomach full of absence.
I sat next to her driving, yelling, "Brakes!"

Time is a rascal magpie, exotic in the corn.
A yogi asked, "What if this baby should die?"
I sit next to her driving, yelling, "Brakes!"
My heart beats audibly past midnight curfew.

A yogi asked, "What if this baby should die?
Her tongue is long." He wrote on his slate at Lama Mountain.
My heart beats audibly past midnight curfew.
At Christ in the Desert I cried in the chapel for loss.

Her tongue is long, he wrote on his slate in silence.
She's kissed a boy she loved and some she didn't.
At Christ in the Desert I cried in the chapel for loss.
I sat with older mothers who had moved on.

She's kissed a boy she loved and some she didn't.
The dark boy leans against his pickup truck.
I sat with older mothers who had moved on.
I say to myself, "Let go. It's not worth creating a tragedy."

SOMETHING LIKE MARRIAGE

I'm engaged to New Mexico. I've been engaged for eighteen years.
I've worn its ring of rainbow set with a mica shard.
I've given my dowry already, my skin texture, my hair moisture.
I've given New Mexico my back East manners. My eyesight.
The arches of my feet.
New Mexico's a difficult fiancé. I learn the word chamisa,
and the plant takes an alias. I say "Indian rice grass,"
New Mexico calls me a racist. I plant trees for it, carry
water to them. At first New Mexico plays hard to get, says,
learn Spanish. Study adobe making. Make hammered tin light
fixtures for the house.
I'm engaged to New Mexico, but I don't want to marry New Mexico.
It's too large. It burps when it drinks beer. It leaves the
toilet seat up. It likes beans cooked with lard and chile so hot

that even people born here and nursed on a chile, can't take the heat.
I tell it, I'll date you, but I don't want to marry you.
You promised, it says, it's been eighteen years. But I was younger.
Now I'm not ready to commit. I've been to Chicago. I've seen
Manhattan next to a man I love. I've dined on Thai food
in Boulder, Colorado. My mother tells me, you could do better.
New Mexico's not good enough for you.
But we're engaged. It gave me these cuticles, these dust devil
eyes and my Bar-None brand. But I have to admit, even to mom,
that I don't love it anymore. Truth to tell, it was infatuation,
never should have gone on so long. I bought rhinestones, and it
threw them to the stars. I bought velvet, and it made velvet
paintings of coyotes.
I want to leave New Mexico, but it acts like it owns me. I only
wear red and black, the secret state colors. I dream New Mexico
license plates on all the cars in eternity. It follows me
everywhere like mesquite cologne, calls me "señorita"
in a loud voice in public.
I love New Mexico in the dark, but I don't want its kisses, full
of prickly pear and rattler. I want an ocean voyage. I want
a real state like Massachusetts, full of Pilgrims, lots of grief
and headlines. I want back my youth. I'm flirting with Alaska.
I've got a bad crush on Wyoming. I'm even pining for my old love,
Pennsylvania. My hope chest is full of turquoise and Chimayó
weavings. They are all dusty and creased with years of waiting.
Dear New Mexico, I write. Meet me in Española at Ranch 'O Casados
at 5 P.M. on Saturday. We have to talk.
It rides into Española on an Appaloosa. It carries a lariat
and ropes me in the Big Rock parking lot. Kiss me darling,
it drawls. Its spurs reverberate.
See what I'm up against?

SOMETHING

Sophia had a secret even Sophia
didn't know. Something about
candles at night, no taste of pork
in her grandmother's house. Something.

Shadowed memory of her grandmother
in her dark bedroom, her voice nearly
a whisper, "It passes down through the women."
That and "Tell your daughter."

Something about the farolitos lined up,
a top to spin. "Our family came from Spain,
not Mexico, hundreds of years ago, you know.
This is your great-grandfather, Israel.

See how handsome he was." Sophia recalls it all,
but mixed with other recollections, the smell
of pine at Christmas, candles on Sunday at mass,
the sight of blood at butchering each fall.

Something about candles to Saint Esther.
It didn't all make sense. "We came here from Spain.
Look hard at this photograph." Her mother's voice
in the kitchen light, flour in the air.

She'd tell her daughters something soon.
She's been meaning to. For hundreds of years.
She'll tell them soon. She will.

THE ANGELS OF PITTSBURGH

The angels of Pittsburgh have no bells in their names.
Pittsburgers swallow final vowels, a strange repast
eaten in immigrant languages. Angels become angls,
losing the very syllable seraphim long to inhabit.

Russian and Polish angels with hands in pockets, slouch,
forget to sing. Working-class angels with drab caps,
jackets full of rebar, steel-toed boots. They smoke.
They love their family, hang out in corner bars.

These are the saddest angels in America, with unspellable
Eastern European names and ethnic foods nobody makes right
anymore. They fought in the war, sit on skeletal skyscrapers,

and Pittsburgh is their Paris, their Berlin.
Andrew Carnegie endowed Pittsburgh. He wanted to grow wings,
meet God. His heaven is an old library next to a museum
with arranged dinosaur bones. He rides ghost streetcars
down Ellsworth, veers left at Craig past a vacant garage.

Takes Fifth Avenue all the way downtown. The conductor,
a sore throat lozenge in his mouth, shouts out stops.
"Museum. Pitt. Children's Hospital. Playhouse. The Hill."
Carnegie pulls the wire to ring the bell, leaving the trolley

full of angels. I've ridden next to sad angels, sodden wings
hidden in suit coats. I was born there, love their grief,
A native of gravity. My mother flew off to groom and bleach,
my father fixed the knot of his necktie in a mirror

inhabited by angels. Whenever I sing, my back
is to East Liberty, my front to the Monongahela.
Three rivers pour out of me, all golden and the Angel
of Learning who lives in Oakland is my voice coach.

I ride the barges with angels, up through the locks,
and they inform me, God has moved back to Pittsburgh
to be among steelworkers who prayed him here.
Unemployed until eternity, they needed him closer.

ANNE   MacNAUGHTON

Writing to Declare My Place in the World

"The subject of my work is 'my place in the world,' as Wendell Berry says; and my locus for the last quarter century has been the southwestern United States. Hence when I write the objective world as it is around me, I write New Mexico. The natural world, the earth herself, is my environment and my influence. I write my life and am a rural person. What I *do* in my life is read, write, paint, draw, raise children, plants, and animals. I farm the land and praise its cycles. 'I live in my subject,' as Berry says, 'and when I am finished writing, I can only return to what I have been writing about.'"

Born in Arkansas and raised in Houston, Anne MacNaughton worked briefly at the Texas State Library as an archivist of historical manuscripts before dropping out of graduate school in 1970 and moving to the Libre artists' community in Colorado, where she started an alternative school and coedited the *Wordworks* literary quarterly. Relocating to northern New Mexico in 1979, she worked an assortment of odd jobs and was an Indian education tutor and an instructor in Taos High School's international education program. Along with Peter Rabbit, she cofounded the Taos Poetry Circus in 1982 and has been a poetry activist ever since. MacNaughton is a visual artist, playwright, and founding member of the Luminous Animal jazz-poetry performance ensemble. Her work has been published in *The Best Poetry of 1989* (Scribners, 1990) and *The Rag and Bone Shop of the Heart* (Harper Collins, 1992), as well as in numerous literary journals and magazines.

"I am affected by the cultures of the native peoples who live on the earth, global communication, oral tradition, and music. These poems are written to be heard. I believe the source of poetry is sound. Brother art to music, poetry originates in mankind's need to make sense of chaos, to order the world, to make magic with sound.

"I believe in the sanctity of the word. By using words as my medium, I acknowledge a sacred responsibility: to be aware—each time I use them—of their meaning and of the terrible power they have to evoke and to create, both well short of and well beyond what I might have intended. I want to use them sparingly, carefully."

MacNaughton resides in Taos.

GOOD GOD GERTIE YOU'RE COOL

There in your black robes,
grand mother and father both
seated in the place reserved
for judgment. Smile
stretched flat
beneath the brow lined
from so much serious
White dog as sweetheart
beneath your hand.
Her portrait on the wall.

Teach me, old lady,
the source of syllable.
We could dream a pure tongue
of such antiquity that each
word would hold
its own history, tell
the time and place of its birth,
first breathing
release into human voice.

Let's start a dialogue
with creation.
Would we so honor
words that we'd remember
how to enter the sacred
   (thus)
            with each speaking?

Word, wort, orth, waúrd.
   Eirein.   Vardas.
Verbum.
Tell, tellen, tolde. Zellen.

Telja. Talthi. Tale.
Tongue, tunga, dingua.
  Tung Wa.

Initial language. Living syntax
where in
each time a word is said
the speaker adds to common
thread phonemic notes.
Gene a logy
of every mouth that's spoken it.

Shall we word it now
from the beginning, Granny?
The poet here
full of words.
And you
in your seat, black
robes, white
dog, the brow lined
with so much
cellular. Syllable.

1ST OF MAY
Keresan Corn Dance

At San Felipe
        watersnake arrives
                macaw feathers at the head
                        eagle feathers flapping
                                babies in tail

Avanyu

crawling into sunken plaza
        millennial dust
                danced down
                        black river mud

---

it coils
around the egg of singers
      drumming
           at the center
           in sweet morning rain

EASTER BREAD

i.

With closed eyes
I roll it out.
With powdered fingers
I feel along it
for evenness.
A tube,
an inch and a half thick
slightly pointed.
It reminds me of
Something.

ii.

The bread, like christ
WILL rise.
Only sometimes,
if the kitchen's very cold
it may take
three days.

iii.

Baguette dough
is better if beaten,
becoming soft, supple
even-tempered
obedient
no big ideas anywhere.

---

iv.

Finished.
The loaves lie
belly up on the table
like long, white fish.

NEW YEAR'S EVE AT HOT SPRINGS RANCH
for Archie Mac

Crystal sky laced
to adobe walls by
            bare cottonwoods.
White stone tank.

Our toes tingle,
            we're up to our necks in mountain water.
Coyotes begin their singing in the silhouette
of a hill. The original party animal.

Let's sit up all night and listen to the earth revolve!
Orion skates across the stars
            Hail pinhead hunter!
                        a whole galaxy at the tip of his penis
                                    pulling a bow he aims straight
                        through the nose of Taurus
                  steady deer dancer
            to grandfather Jupiter's
shining ojo
wearing the Pleiades as a cap.

                  Dance.
            Dance.
Dance, you Mogollon drums!
            The rock walls here have crumbled
                  & we're down to ocote
                                    cholla
                        hummingbird moth
            & hot water.

E.   A.   M A R E S

Family, Tradition, History

In exile from his native New Mexico, E. A. Mares continues to write fiction, poetry, and plays in Denton, Texas, where he teaches at the University of North Texas. After growing up in Albuquerque's Old Town, E. A. Mares went on to become a distinguished scholar of history, a man of letters, a performer who brought to life one of the key figures in New Mexico history, Padre Antonio José Martínez of Taos. His most recent book is a collection of poems, *The Unicorn Poem and Flowers and Songs of Sorrow* (West End Press, 1992). He is also known for his historical writing, as in Alex Traube and E. A. Mares, *Las Vegas, New Mexico: A Portrait* (University of New Mexico Press, 1984).

"Always in the background of my earliest years is the figure of my powerful grandmother. Spiritually, she was a direct descendant of all those elderly women in black shawls who populate the churches of Spain and Latin America. In a sense, I was born into Latin America, but it took me many years to realize this. My grandmother believed that through prayer and the intercession of the saints you could influence the course of the weather, human events, and the making of history itself.

"Unfortunately, there were many negative features of my early education. I was frequently silenced, intimidated, by the authoritarian religious figures of my early education. But I was not convinced....An eccentric like Florinto, a rag and bone man from my childhood, or the kindly Padre Goni, a Jesuit priest fresh from Spain, hinted that the world was large, enigmatic, fascinating. I accepted what I could not change as a child and lived, psychologically speaking, to fight another day.

"There is now and always will be a deep love in me for New Mexico. It is forever a part of my creative process. At the same time, I am saddened by the cheapening of New Mexico...the brightly painted and decorated plywood tepees in Gallup, the new Santa Fe pandering after the nouveaux riches while its locals suffer, the economic poverty and contradictions one sees everywhere in the state.

"For all I know, I may never again live in New Mexico. This is an unbearable thought, but I know it may be true. However, wherever I travel, something of New Mexico travels with me."

ROLLING THROUGH THE COUNTRY OF NOUNS

I drive through the country of nouns.
Earth, sky, sun, mountain.
These hard-edged paintings
Austere as White Sands
Or the plains west of Amarillo,
Then the Sandia Mountains,
Come slowly up to horizon
As I drive west.

Once my distant cousin Juan Mares
Wandered the Red River country for years
As a "guest" of the Comanches.
He was trying to get back to Santa Fe,
Trying to find or keep a faith
That lived up to the abstract noun
Sufficient, in any case, to sustain him.

Up ahead on Highway 287
Are the nouns of road survival:
Love's, Stucky's, coffee, gas
Jerky with driedredchile
Or driedgreenchile
(Both are nouns),
Whiskey and its burn,
Then the motel bed
At the "Ranchouse,"
Pronounced "Ranchoose," I suppoose,

Or at the "It'll Do" motel,
And I understand.
"It'll do" just fine
For these, my down times.
Nothing is sharp or clear.
I need to rest, to prepare the hard nouns,
The obsidian-tipped arrows
I mean to shoot into the next century.

These images hang from the mental page
Like paintings from the Hard Edge School
On the bare walls of an art museum.
My cousin Juan Mares
Eventually made it back to Santa Fe.

Rolling through the country of nouns,
I need more than a good jeep
To get there.
I guess I'll just keep driving.

BENT'S FORT*

On the north bank
of the Arkansas River,
Bent's Fort
looks to the south.

The northern archer
takes aim to the south,
making a target of the "x"

in Mexico.

Today the tourists
visit Bent's Fort.
After a while, exhausted,

---

*Bent's Fort, in the state of Colorado, United States, was the point of departure for the
American troops under the command of Colonel Kearny for the invasion of Mexico in 1846.

---

they yawn from reading too much
about Kit Carson and Charles Bent.
A child cries
because he wants to take a piss.

He wants to make water
right here on history.
Yes, child, I think to myself.
I understand.

BENT'S FORT*

En las orillas
del lado norte del río Arkansas
Bent's Fort
mira hacia el sur.

El arquero del norte
apunta al sur,
haciendo blanco del "x"

de México.

Hoy los turistas
visitan Bent's Fort.
Al fin se cansan,

bostejan de leer tanto
de Kit Carson y Carlos Bent.
Un niño llora
porque quiere mearse.

El quiere hacer orines
aquí en la historia.
Sí niño, pienso yo.
Lo entiendo.

*Bent's Fort, estado de Colorado, EEUU, fue el punto de partida de las tropas norteamericanas
bajo el mando del coronel Kearny para invadir a México en 1846.

BAR CHINERE

The people in Guiana
Say "Chinere," to mean
"Lo Que Dios Me Ha Dado"—
"What God Has Given Me."

On the Calle de León, Madrid,
I drink at the Bar Chinere—
What God Has Given Me.

This is Africa in Madrid
Not far from the Prado,
Darkness and light in your eyes.
The blaring green neon sign

Starkly proclaims
"Bar Chinere,"
"What God Has Given Me,"
In the Spanish night.

It could be a rural church in the Midwest,
Or more likely in Texas or New Mexico,
Con una cantina al lado,
The faithful attending the service
In the temple of their choice.

But we are here in Madrid,
The old Moorish campsite,
Mannichean city of clashing faiths.
I am a man from the mountain escarpments
And you are African with turquoise eyes.

Large and bloody forceps
Pulled me screaming into this
My twentieth century.
I think of the International Brigades.
Anarchist and socialist songs
Trip easily off my tongue.

And the old faith rekindles.
Beneath red and black banners

We will dance, hands clasped
Together across all frontiers.

Here in Madrid, the Bar Chinere,
This is What God Has Given Me!
Lo Que Dios Me Ha Dado.
I'll drink to that.

DEMETRIA MARTINEZ

Returning Home by Leaving

"The paradox of my three years in Kansas City is that my writing there was defined by my relationship to New Mexico. First, I left New Mexico because a private life—the solitude needed for writing—became impossible even after my trial for smuggling refugees ended. Second, when I came to Kansas City, I discovered the poems I'd written in New Mexico during the previous eight years were actually rough drafts for what became my first novel, *Mother Tongue*, set in Albuquerque (Bilingual Press/Editorial Bilingue, 1994)."

Born and raised in Albuquerque, Demetria Martinez received her B.A. in 1982 from the Woodrow Wilson School of Public and International Affairs at Princeton, where she was a Wilson Scholar and studied poetry with Maxine Kumin and Stanley Kunitz. Following a stint as religion writer for the *Albuquerque Journal*, she moved to the Kansas City-based *National Catholic Reporter*, where she worked as national news editor. Currently, she lives in Tucson, where she is a columnist for the *Reporter*.

"I have frequently explored what I call 'the poetry of reporting and the reporting within poetry,'" Martinez says. In 1988, in a celebrated Sanctuary case, she was indicted on federal charges of smuggling Salvadoran refugees into the United States. Following a two-week trial, she was found innocent on First Amendment grounds; the jury concluded she had acted within her rights as a reporter while she accompanied a minister who aided two Salvadoran women on their 1986 journey across the U.S.-Mexico border and into the United States.

"As I work on my second novel, *Mexican Rubies*, from the distance of Tucson, I find it allows me a way to go home—to Santa Fe, a place I could never afford to live, even if I wanted to. And when the words don't come, I make poems about New Mexico, adobe bricks of the imagination, then add those to the house which is the novel.

"I worry that if I ever moved back to New Mexico, I might not be able to write about it. I prefer my memories, real and imagined. If I saw it too close up, I might not be able to see the spirits that dwell behind the cliches: the coyotes and *ristras*, the O'Keeffes and New Agers. On the other hand, I know I'll move back—to rediscover my home, to make its geography mine again. But until that time, I have to return by going within."

Martinez's collection of poetry, *Turning*, received a first place prize for poetry in the 14th Annual Chicano Literary Contest sponsored by the University of California. *Turning* was published by Bilingual Press/Editorial Bilingue, 1989, as part of a collection entitled *Three Times a Woman: Chicana Poetry*.

ONLY SAY THE WORD

A Poem for Three Women's Voices (an excerpt)

"Only Say the Word" takes place at the Santuario de Chimayó, a nineteenth-century Catholic church built by Spanish colonists in northern New Mexico. In a room attached to the main sanctuary is a small hollow of earth believed to possess healing properties. Another adjoining room contains crutches, canes, and written testimonies of miraculous healings. Each year thousands visit the Santuario de Chimayó. They kneel around the hollow, cross themselves with the earth, and take handfuls home with them.

Pilgrims also venerate a crucifix called Our Lord of Esquípulas, which is similar to that found at the church of Esquípulas in Guatemala. According to legend, Spaniards found the cross buried in the earth at Chimayó. Many miraculous events took place there, and they built their church over that hollow of earth which is venerated today.

Long before the Spaniards built the Santuario, Pueblo Indians believed the earth in the Chimayó Valley possessed curative powers. The Indians had many legends about the area. One says that a fight between a monster and some Pueblo gods caused fire and water to emerge from the site where the Santuario stands today.

"Only Say the Word" is about three women: a Guatemalan Indian, a North American schoolteacher, and a Chimayó native.

First Voice:
> Our father who art in heaven,
> Hallowed be thy name,
> Thy Kingdom come,
> Thy will be—
>
> Our father who art in heaven,
> Hallowed be thy name,
> Thy Kingdom
> Come—
>
> How many times have I said this prayer?
> How many Sundays have the people of Cordero,
> My village, held hands at Mass
> Begging you, Lord, "Líbranos del mal,"
> Deliver us from evil?
>
> It does not work,
> The prayer does not work.
> The words turn to stone in my mouth.
> I must find new words
> Now, or I will choke.
> I must make a new prayer
> The way a woman makes new soup
> From yesterday's bones.
>
> If the old prayer tires you, Lord,
> Be patient.
> I will salt and stir my words,
> A brew so bitter,
> You cannot resist forever,
> You will hear, God,
> You will answer.
>
> Wood, wood and ash:
> These are the colors of the people
> In Cordero.
> We are dark but lovely,
> Strong, though now broken.
> We live in shadows of guns and jeeps,
> One by one we are disappeared.
> Guards in green uniforms,

Like statues come to life, terrify.
After Mass one Sunday
They tore our saints out of niches,
Smashed our chalices,
Threw lots for altar cloths
Our grandmothers wove.

My husband learned to read the Bible,
He memorized the book of Luke.
After a day in the coffee plantations
Neighbors would gather to pray,
To hear my husband read:
"Bienaventurados los pobres,"
Blessed are the poor,
The Kingdom will be ours.

Then, ten men,
No older than seventeen,
The gleam of the devil
In their yellow eyes,
They beat my husband with rifles
Until his face
Was a bloody moon.

I fell on top of him,
I thought he was dead.
Neighbors' cries, like those of dogs
Tortured for fun, rose to heaven,
No guardian angels landed.

My husband lives, but cannot smell
The steam of tortillas and black beans,
Nor the scent of the body
Which bore his four children.
He calls me his "rosa,"
But what is a rose without scent?
A paper flower, flat,
Which no one will buy.
Fear, like a fruit pit,
Is lodged in my husband's throat.
He chokes in his sleep, weeps,
Speaks about escaping to the north.

Where is our help,
Christ, Messiah,
Born of a woman who made love
With life?
Must strife be our hated spouse,
Beating us?

Come down off that cross!
That thorny crown is heavy,
You have not lifted your head
In 2,000 years,
Eyes closed through
Earthquake, hunger, war.
Nails at your hands and feet,
Rusty, bloody.
Your skin, brown and burnt like mine,
But you are numb.

You were once a troublemaker.
Like a woman with a broom
In a filthy house,
You whipped the temple clean
Of greedy men.
Hungry, you picked corn
From another man's fields.
Thirsty, you turned water into wine.

Come down off that cross:
Or we'll call on our old gods,
Give us this day our daily breath,
Deliver us from mad men's claws.

Second Voice:
Hail Mary, full of grace...
Mother to an impossible boy,
Your son's words blinded many,
His touch made the blind see.
I have forgotten how to pray.
Prayers, like nursery rhymes
And rattles, seem quaint, impotent.
A Christmas and Easter thing to do,
Like buying new shoes.
What do people say here, kneeling?

I do not know how to pray.
But I do know that when a child
Wants a favor from the father
She goes to the mother.
So I ask you, please, pray for me,
Our heavenly father has turned from me.

My student, Loretta, 15 years old,
Due in a month with twins.
I knew of her pregnancy before she did.
Conception casts a spell upon the young.
Her face grew moist,
Her sentences, fragmented.
Odors of roses, rain, came off her
As she panted into class, late.
She listened to lectures but did not hear,
Her eyes glistened like full moons.
Her essays are luminous,
She could be a scientist.
She's found a cure
For loneliness in the crucible
Of her womb.

I have taught world history
For twenty-four years.
When I was young I imagined that books
Were scaffolding about students' faces,
That teachers could restore sight.
Children might see that hate,
War, and greed are futile,
Useless as prayers to Zeus.

I'm older now, I say less,
I show slides on a screen, instead.
Of soap chunks Nazis made
With human fat,
Negatives of bodies on Nagasaki's walls,
Children's faces torn by napalm,
Their bones, little trellises
For mankind's sins.

I have taught thousands
And have helped no one.

My words, like leaves
a fountain, decay.
can I possibly say to Loretta,
child turned mother
one day to the next?

Her parents fight about money each week,
Histories of wars are nothing to her.
Valuable paintings cover the family's walls,
Like the alcohol her father consumes,
Like her mother's endless good causes:
Investments against the elements,
Loveless, sterile.
Loretta has all she wants,
Nothing she needs.

She is a fortress now,
Imperturbable.
Two hearts beating in her womb,
Two pairs of eyes and legs.
If not twins, it would be tumors
Growing, filling her empty spaces.
The body does not know the difference
When there is coldness, emptiness.

In twenty-four years
I have changed nothing.
Hope falls about me like
Chipped paint from the classroom ceiling.
At times I sit, a paralytic.
Books, teaching awards look down at me
Like disappointed parents
With nothing to say
About how to bear on.

Third Voice:
You women have wept too long
In the sanctuary,
There are tree rings around your eyes,
A ring for each year of grief.
Such wintry, leafless expressions.
You are not accountable
For the sorrows hurled at you.

A terrible rust is loose
In rain, in soil, in hearts.
Those who do not hold the gun
Are killed by the bullet,
The rest look on, indifferent.

You hold your hands
To your children's ears,
Hoping they will not hear
The terrifying report.
What more can any man
Or woman do?

Why I am blessed with safety,
With happiness, I do not know.
I was baptized, confirmed
And married at this altar.
The town of Chimayó
Is as familiar to me as water.
My husband and boy raise cattle,
We run a small store.

I sat in bed last night by an open window,
Watching cottonwoods collect
Stars in leafy nets.
Scents of sweet grass and hay
From my husband's body filled me.
I walked along the road this morning,
Sunlight turned Chimayó's stuccoed walls
Into copper and gold.
My grey hairs turned gold.
I am rich, very rich:
No boot has kicked open my door at night,
Sadness does not splinter my heart.

Each year thousands visit this church.
During Holy Week by car, on foot,
Like salmon twisting upstream
Returning to the place of birth, they come:
Cold, easterly winds cannot stop them.
Purses, pockets swell with rosaries
And plastic bags.
They hear Mass, they line up

To enter the room with "la tierra bendita,"
A room with a pit of sacred earth.
They place it on their tongues
And in bags to take home.
Stories of miraculous healings
Are strewn about like seeds in wind.
Each year a few more crutches and canes
Hang from hooks on the wall,
Useless as old calendars.

Something happens to people in this church,
Though they themselves do not always see it.
Hair and skin smell of incense, candle wax,
Eyes, like lakes on a still day,
Look to the sun, unflinching.
Praying can alter the body
As much as the soul.
Lines that life chisels into faces
For a moment fade.
They may not know it
But they have made love.

I have said enough.
You women must enter the room,
And kneel before the sacred pit.
It is dark but lovely.
Like the *sipapu* of a Pueblo Kiva,
It is a hole leading
To the center of the earth.
Once it yielded fire and smoke.
It grows larger as you look,
Like a woman dilating before birth.

Rub the earth into your palms,
Scars on your lifelines will fade.
Rub the earth into your lips,
Your words will emblazon neighbor and student,
As for your enemies, your wisdom
Is poison.
Come in now: It is sin to think all is hopeless,
Those who say you are helpless will die.

MARY McGINNIS

Cultivating Space and Stillness

Photo: Steve Cottage

"**B**eing on the land grounds me so I can write about all my obsessions. Images from the land—textures, colors, sounds, scents—find their way into my work. Fragments of Spanish turn up in my poems when I least expect them. The subtleties of different kinds of desert grasses and the air in the desert at different seasons are most clarified for me when I'm writing in solitude....I do many first drafts of poems outdoors, sitting on a patio made of desert stones, sitting on an old, weathered wooden box, on the ground under juniper trees in sun or in shade, with a wool cap on my head when it's winter and I still want to be in the fresh air."

Mary McGinnis has lived in New Mexico since 1972. She has taught writing classes for women with disabilities, baked and sold bread, and now works in Santa Fe at her local independent living center as a counselor, educator, and trainer. Her life and writing have been influenced by the desert, the women's movement, and the disability rights movement. Her poetry has been published in various anthologies and magazines, such as *Women of Power*, *New American Review*, and *Disability Rag*. In 1988, she self-published her chapbook *Private Stories on Demand*.

"I give myself lots of empty time before I start writing—time during which I might be meditating, resting, daydreaming, listening to piñon jays, courting the first lines or thoughts of a poem, doing nothing but being open to their arrival. During the creation of the first draft, I write very fast. I don't worry about line breaks or whether what I am writing will turn out to be a poem....I cultivate the same space and stillness to revise my poems....I might reenter a first draft soon after writing it if I have an intuition about

where the writing and I can go together. On the other hand, it might be
months or years before I'm ready to go back to a piece to revise or discard."

McGinnis resides in Santa Fe.

DESERT STONES TALKING

When it's this hot,
and you hear thunder in the mountains,
the thunder will sound

the way stones would if they could talk,
their gray tongues
making a noise

they stole from the sky,
a sound of longing
that rolls and rolls

across people's necks and ears,
a sound that isn't a word
asking for water—

it will make you sweat,
and stop talking
in the middle of a sentence;

everything waits for the storm to come:
stones have that waiting
in their hard turtle backs,

and if they could speak,
they would say one of three words:
"live," "die," "now"

and if you were planning on talking to stones,
the only words you should say to them
would be

Yes or No.
Their voices are like hammers,
like the twisted curves of wood

that was warped by the sun;
they have the voices of junipers
giving out fragrance

when it's 95 degrees.
Listen to them;
Listen to them;
they are telling you about emptiness,

and beginning again
and about living
on nothing.

READING BRAILLE

It wasn't my stomach that liked to read, but those socially acceptable
    parts:
the orderly hands, the thin shapely wrists, the neck with its pockets of
    deceit,
the mouth with its tiny partitions, the eyes with their flower centers;
it wasn't the nose, it wasn't the legs in their sheathes of skin,

the ankle bones that protruded—it was the head,
the brain with its secret lobes,
the spine with its little curvatures;
all of these parts read and read when I was a child,
these parts with their clear black and white English names, not

la cabeza, o los manos o los ojos,
o la cara o las piedras o la primavera blanca;
not the knee but the fingertips, not the thigh but the petite ear;
all of me sank into my lap where the book was;
they talked about the ambulance coming, about my great aunts who were
    sick;
my mother talked on the phone about what the hairdresser said about
    sex,

my father answered my mother in mumbled syllables over the blare of
    the television,
and I sat very still on the couch so they wouldn't notice
that I hadn't gone to bed;

I read and dreamed of wild, dark places near the water,
pearl divers who dove for pearls and had seaweed on their arms;
I was not at home in my body then,
and I read until my fingers were raw, and there were
words racing through my head and I didn't have to talk
or ask too many questions.
I loved the quiet in the house when my parents were sleeping—
when I was alone with my hands.

THINGS MY MOTHER MUST HAVE SAID

Let her live. Let her have
my dark hair, but give it more curl.

Give her my good skin. Make sure she has my thrift,
my hands, my small feet.

Make her into a teacher; don't let her
tramp through the world, trying to sell the world.

Have her faithful, have her marry, have her iron.
Show her how to do wallpaper, show her how to do

whatever is needed. Teach her about whole-wheat bread,
and cleaning Venetian blinds. Help her learn to swim.

Give her a steady hand, a back and neck that endure,
and let her dance some, stand behind a counter,

reeling them in with her smile. Give her a few
of her father's brains; he's so smart he won't miss them;

not his crazy, stumbling feet, or how he drives a car.
And squeeze his wayward singing back into the dark

from where it came. And leave out my silliness,
how I could fall in love without good reasons.
Bring her out of me—on time and perfect.
Leave her a clock in her head so she'll never be late.

Straighten her shoulders if she falters.
Make a mixture of him and me in her bones,
but more than the two of us.
Make her a sunny child who picks up her clothes.

C A R O L   M O L D A W

Photo: Mariana Cook

Over Time, Memory Turns
into Imagination

"I lived in New Mexico for two years before any of its landscape or my experiences here found their way into a poem. It's as if the impressions have to seep down deep enough until they are absorbed into my system, and then my imagination feels free, unconstrained. Over time, memory turns into imagination."

Carol Moldaw was born in Oakland, California, and was raised in the San Francisco Bay Area. In 1979, she graduated cum laude from Harvard-Radcliffe. Moldaw's poetry has appeared in the *New Republic*, the *New Yorker*, the *Kenyon Review*, *FishDrum*, and many other publications. Her poetry book, *Taken from the River*, was published in 1993 (Alef Books). Before moving to Pojoaque, New Mexico, she was a teaching fellow in the Creative Writing Program at Boston University, where she studied with Derek Walcott and received her M.A. Moldaw is a 1994 recipient of a National Endowment for the Arts fellowship.

"Time is often a crucial element in the emergence of my poems," she writes. "Often I have felt that I *must* write a poem to understand or explore or describe something I have just seen or thought or experienced, but I cannot write the poem close in time to that perception. Years might pass. The thing will come and go in my mind. I will write down words, descriptions, associations, but something doesn't click. The specific music of the poem hasn't appeared yet, and until it does, all the good intentions in the world, all the diligence, will not create that poem—though they are necessary, too. Faith is especially necessary.

"I like the sense of open space in New Mexico, the vastness of the horizon, the shocking nuances of color in the earth, and the bright liveliness of the sky....I like the way the greens are weathered, patinated, faded, deep, but rarely bright. Green here is something to be savored, or to be gobbled, but it is not a staple. Everything here is alive. Death is alive."

BEADS OF RAIN

Each day I've looked
into the beveled mirror
on this desk, vainly
asking it questions
reflection cannot answer.

Outside, fog and frost
and silver olive leaves.
I can see at most
a half field's depth,
then the trees are lost
in the gauzy mist
like thin unbraceleted arms
swallowed by billowing sleeves.

I'd like to face
that stringent looking glass
transparent to myself
as beads of rain
pooled on a green leaf.

But ever self-composed
in self-regard,
and my eyes opaque
as a dancer's leotard,
to see straight through myself
I need what love supplies:
its dark arrows, dear,
not its white lies.

OUR NEW LIFE

If the field is thick
with horse shit and the garden
unplanted, and the roof
needs repair; if after the next storm
sand from the acequia
overflows and suffocates the marsh,
killing the cattails where redwinged blackbirds nest,
if the neighbors' horses overgraze our field,
if I am lonely,
if a WIPP truck overturns
going back and forth from Los Alamos
to the shifting salt pits in Carlsbad,
if we go away for a week
and miss the crab apple's blossoming,
the sheep shearing,
if it turns out I am allergic to Russian olives,
to chamisa, to rabbit grass,
if they pave our dirt road,
if the cat returns to her original owner,
if the walls need remudding after every storm,
if the doctor finds a problem,
if the beer cans and corn chip bags and whiskey bottles
pile up on the road
faster than we can collect them for the dump,
if the doctor doesn't know what is wrong,
if Los Alamos gets the contract
to manufacture or stockpile or do anything whatever
with nuclear warheads,
if I cut my foot on a rusty washing machine part
while walking down by the river,
if I get lost in the Barrancas,
if my heart keeps shrinking,
if my heart explodes—
will I ever again think to look
for the new moon's thinnest crescent,
will we ever crane our necks together,
as we used to, name the stars,
turn down the cool sheets,
go to bed not exhausted,
arms linked in one constellation
that turns all night in synch with the sky?

SUMMER SUBLET

Sunlight sharp enough to slice
black-eyed Susans from their stems,
to sliver stone, so that a wall,
unmortared, laid with river rock
and slab, shimmers in the heat.

But once inside, the flagstone chills
like a gin and tonic, like when
you chew the cubes, and I shiver.
At noon, it's too dark to read a book
without a lamp, too dark to tell

the scalloped tin retablo of Mary
that leans on the corner fireplace mantel
from Grandma's hand-colored tintypes
taken and saved from the shtetl.
I lie on my side on the bed and read,

or else I sit at the all-purpose table,
make phone calls, and look out the window.
"One day at a time," my neighbor's car,
parked on the narrow washboard road,
reminds me. "One day at a time."

I watch him string a ristra, red
electric chilies, from his door.
In Asia, he also strung lights, something
electronic, a civilian during war.
He showed me a room in his landlord's house,

a room without floor or ceiling,
the windows strafed with bullet holes
where someone tried to collect on a debt.
The room was in back where the house had sunk.
Testing a warped board with my toe,

I placed my hot plate, desk, and shelves,
before coming to, and saying no.
These rooms are either one step up
or one down, and circuit endlessly
around the central storage space.

New York's as far as Kiev, except
I call, except, like Katmandu,
this is a place the world treks through.
Our sublet's a house of ghosts, mostly
not ours. Not mine, the bearded dead

boyfriend whose photo's enshrined on a shelf,
with matches, a candle for us to light;
not mine, the broken violin,
or yours, the tongue depressor cross,
the shards of Anasazi pots,

the freezer full of bread and bones.
Stacks of postcards, like playing cards,
leaning against books we've never read,
with love from people we haven't met,
are collecting dust we'll never dust.

We lie face up on the half-made bed
while summer makes the most of us.
July breaks on our windowsill.
We're awash in its salty marinade
till August sears us on the grill.

LINDA MONACELLI-JOHNSON

**Even the Architecture
Smells of History**

Linda Monacelli-Johnson was born in Pittsburgh, Pennsylvania, and grew up in Cleveland, Ohio. She received her B.A. from Saint Mary's College (Notre Dame, Indiana) and her M.A. from Cleveland State University—both in English literature. She has lived in New Mexico since 1977 and works as a free-lance writer and editor.

"I love the way Santa Fe's architec-ture even smells of history. The land-scape also thrills me. Though I grew up in Cleveland, I feel most at home in this high desert with mountains all around. Living for a decade in Tesuque prompted me to focus more and more on the landscape. Meeting and marry-ing a landscape painter who is also an avid camper fostered my growing interest in nature. Poetry has become a way for me to explore nature, and nature has grounded my poetry, even poems with other subjects."

Monacelli-Johnson's first book, *Lacing the Moon*, was published in 1978 by the Cleveland State University Poetry Center. In 1986, her second book, *Weathered*, was published by Sunstone Press. Her poems have been translated into Italian and published in Italy, as well as in literary magazines and an-thologies throughout the United States.

"I have also come to realize that painting landscapes and writing nature poetry are two ways of affirming natural beauty and bounty, which have become more and more threatened. Such affirmation is metaphysical support for any practical steps toward environmental restoration and preservation."

SITTINGS FOR WHITMAN

i

He begins painting in the lightest mizzle;
a small study of her lolling
against a hillside tree won't take long
if it doesn't really rain. With her clunky

hiking boots sprawling in the stony
foreground, she leans back into the aroma
of ponderosa and listens to the distant *om*
of cows in pastures below.

ii

They climb to the spring. Beneath
a huge spruce are countless cone
fragments, a mulch fallen from years
of squirrel foraging. She enters

the shaderoom defined by the wingspread
of old branches and lies down with knees bent,
squirms into the natural mattress
so it contours her back, her head, even the knot
in the scarf that wraps her hair. Water seeps

out beside him as he paints. Her eyes rove
the tree's underside,
pulling blue and white through gaps
in evergreen. She spots the sun
at intervals, gauging its perches
to see how much the earth has moved.

iii

Back home, on the deck, she sits too straight
in a chair. Though they're not in town,
they're not in the country, either. Trucks
on the nearby highway, a cement
mixer somewhere, a neighbor's hammering pester
like persistent insects. A student band concert
begins on the playground of the valley's
elementary school. In unison
the band plays patriotic

songs, each followed by applause.
He draws all the while. When he picks

up his watercolors, she sees the metal paint box
she had as a kid. There are gray strands
in his beard and streaks in her hair. His practiced
hand darts, a dragonfly, from paper towel to water
bottle to paints to painting; the sequence
sometimes varies. As she sits, an iridescence
plays in her head, like children of wind and light
on the schoolyard's multicolored
jungle gym, seesaw, swings, and slide.

CAMP ROBBERS

Thirteen miles to Spirit
Lake and back—the peak
of aspen change and a sky of rapture

inspire us to hike. Leaves shiver;
wind frees the brightest yellow kites.
From pines and blue spruce

come calls that follow
your knapsack; part
of our lunch is a tithe

to gray jays. At the mountain lake
these half-tame creatures train
us to hold a pinch of bread

between thumb and index,
the other three fingers extended,
a perch.

CUNDIYO WILLOWS

i
The ground beneath the weave
of this old willow: a kind
seat in July. Slightly moist,
the earth has absorbed smoke
from a forest fire
in mountains not too far
from this river's thunder.
In the dim hollow
of a fragrant basket
I wonder about the blaze
left to burn itself out.

ii
Ice muffles
the river's music
here and there; yet, bare willows
dance a red waltz
when a breeze whisks
through the canyon. I approach
where the walls quit,
framing sky and valley:
volcanic cinders scattered
on the road, which parody the blush
of pliant willows beyond; a blond
field; snow that mottles
evergreen foothills and dark
blue mountains; a magpie
for a moment.

Poet, Potter, Pueblo Indian Woman—the Human Being I Will Become Tomorrow

Photo: Cate Gilles

"In the Tewa language, there is no word for art. There is, however, the concept for an artful life, filled with inspiration and fueled by labor and thoughtful approach.

"From the moment I wake from sleep, I am continuously absorbing experiences that constitute my life and help to design the human being I will become tomorrow. From immersing my hands into warm dishwater to lifting my feet in rhythm as ancient songs celebrate my native history, I am incorporating sensations into my being; and from these sensations I call gifts, the inspiration to create emerges. When I write, I am simply releasing my life experiences onto open, blank pages, which upon review, reflect all observations, frustrations, dreams, and longings that I feel moved to record.

"At times I catch myself thinking in short poetic form. When this happens, no matter where I am, I reach into the cave of my purse to find the instruments...pencils, broken crayons, envelopes, anything that will help me capture what I have begun to create. Words, phrases, even primitive drawings spill onto the paper...codes that only I am capable of translating, as I learn about myself in the context of this wondrous, wondrous world."

Living on the edge of Santa Clara Pueblo, Nora Naranjo-Morse creates highly acclaimed clay sculptures that blend traditional and modern styles. In her outstanding book *Mud Woman: Poems from the Clay* (University of Arizona Press, 1992), she explores the creative process of working with clay through the medium of poetry. As she says, "the process of recording my life through clay and poetry results in an exciting volley of creative expression for me. Three-dimensional clay pearlenes were often inspired by poems written months or even years before. In return, poems initiate the formulation of images, complete with personality, physical detail, and motive."

Electricity
  down my arm
  through this clay
  forming into
  spirit shapes
    of men
      women
      and children
      I have seen
      somewhere before.

Electricity
  surging upward
  as I mix
  this mud
  like my mother
    as her mother did
    with small
    brown feet.

Folding into this earth
  a decision of
  joyful play,
  transcending expectations
  of fear
    failure
    or perfection.

Creating spirits
  calling invitations
  of celebration.
  What occurs
  in completed form,
  bright
    and bold,
    is motion
    from our mother's skin.

I smile
  momentarily satisfied
  with my play.
  Electricity,
  generated from star colors
  far from home,
  entering
    through my feet
    blessing my hands
    and opening my heart.

THERE IS NOTHING LIKE AN IDEA

There is nothing
  like an idea
    that comes to life
      through clay.
Each step
  a personal investment of
    thought
      labor
        and time.
Hands
  moving quickly,
    rounding curves
      setting up in clay
    skillful responses
      educated
        by Gia's
          simple instruction
            and immense knowledge
              of her own work.
Letting dreams come true
  from songs
    born from within,
      sounds
        inviting irresistible challenges.
There is nothing like an idea
  that comes to life

through clay.
There is nothing better than a life
   whose dreams
      and ideas are
         just too
            impossible
               to resist.

THE LIVING EXHIBIT UNDER THE MUSEUM'S PORTAL

Arriving with high hopes on a breezy March day
      to sell these forms I've made from clay.
      My pocketbook empty, as I lay my blanket down.
We arrive from all directions:
         Cochiti,
            Zuni,
               The Navajo
                  and Pueblos.
Selling our blankets,
      bread
         and beads.
We bargain back and forth with tourists,
      and among ourselves...
      we must love to bargain.
My friend from Zuni tells me business is slow,
      as she keeps her hands busy, rearranging
      necklaces in single file, on black polyester.
      "Damn," she says, "to think, I could be sitting
      in a warm office right this minute, drinking
      hot chocolate and typing business letters
      for some honky."
A tourist and potential customer blurts out:
      "Excuse me, but do any of you Indians speak English?"
      I answer too politely, hating myself for doing so,
      thinking it must be my empty pocketbook
      talking for me.
The Indian tribes represented, line quietly against the stark,
      white museum wall, as each new day introduces
      throngs of tourists, filing past our blankets

fixed in orderly fashion upon red bricks.
Visitors looking for mementos to take home,
that will remind them of the curiously
silent Indians, wrapped tightly in colorful
shawls, just like in the postcards.
Huddling together for warmth, we laugh, remembering
that sexy redhead last summer, who
bent down to pick up a necklace and
ripped her tight white pants.
Casually interested, we watch as Delbert, a city Indian,
hiding behind mirrored sunglasses,
pulls up at noon, to lay his blanket down.
He's come to sell brass and silver
earcuffs he and his girlfriend made.
Delbert sets up, while in the truck
his girlfriend sleeps off last night's party.
My friend is right, business is slow as the late afternoon breeze
hurries customers away from our blankets,
toward the Indian art galleries,
leaving us to feel the sting of cold
through layers of our woolen protection.
The sun fades into the southwestern corner of the plaza
casting large, cold shadows that signal
the end of our day together.
Quietly we pack for home, bundling our wares
carefully in baskets and old grocery crates.
Back to:
 Cochiti,
  Zuni,
   The Navajo
    and Pueblos.
Tomorrow we will arrive, again with high hopes,
empty pocketbooks
          and our friendships right in place.

TOWA

Before communities of strangers settled,
marking Pueblo boundaries

---

and changing the arid
open landscape forever,
there were the people of Black Mesa,
   who called themselves Towa.
People whose clear, brown eyes witnessed
star explosions high above them,
against a celestial canvas of darkness.
The Towa were filled with mystery,
   wonder
      and reverence
         for the universe encircling them.
Reverence gave birth to ritual,
celebration wove ceremony
into songs that blanketed the village
with life-giving spirit.
Planting nourishment for the children of Puye,
with steady handwork,
bedding seeds of corn,
   squash
      and beans.
Drum beats pounded upward,
introducing a new season's fertile ground.
Nimble fingers pressing seedlings into earth beds,
Digging,
   planting,
      covering and smoothing
         in perpetual motion,
            connecting each Towa
               to the cycle of plant life.
From the heavens, to the rain-drenched earth beds,
to the seedlings ripened into colored corn.
From the harvest to the Corn Dance.
Clay-skinned people,
danced with willowlike movements,
then melted quietly into waiting earth beds.
Seedlings creating another
   and yet another of these Towa.
The plant and human life cycle,
   equal in symmetry.
This was before change disrupted night's mystery
and other world views crowded into Pueblo boundaries.
Now Towa rush to their jobs outside of village walls,

adapting to standards unlike their own.
Dressing our clay-skinned bodies
in image-conscious fashion,
we stroke this new life of comfort.
Yet, somewhere in us,
    persistent sounds surge upward
    reminding us of our life cycles,
      and the innocent wonder
        that is our birthright,
          as children of the Towa.

ONE ADOBE AT A TIME

We coiled each row with mud bricks,
    lifting,
      measuring,
        shaping one adobe at a time.
This earth vessel
    rounded into rooms
      we raise our children in.
Staggered bricks of straw
    mud and sand
    like the Towa before us
    who sculpted
    their own shelters
    upward
    in basic
      uneven layers
        one adobe at a time.
In our vessel
    there are thousands of adobes
    anchored to a solid bed of concrete,
    evenly distributing the weight
    of walls seventeen feet high.
Greg designed
    our cradle of packed earth,
    keeping with the adobe tradition
    of simple,
      wavering lines,

that move quietly,
        curving in and out of rooms
            one after another.
Plastering,
        molding
            and repacking
                an endless supply of bricks,
                until our mud shell
                stood upright
                massive
                        and invincible.
Sounds easily surrender
        to walls absorbing
            the details of our lives.
        Coughs from sick children
            romantic whispers
                and heated debates,
                all digested into
                    porous layers of mortar.
I shake my head thinking,
        "Only earth mother
        would permit such a burden,
        allowing us to dig foundations
        into her skin
        and forgiving us the weight
        of tons and tons of mass,
        yet, holding us safe and steady."
        Our vessel made from
            her brown
                solid skin.
                Earth mother,
                giving all that she is,
                    one adobe at a time.

S I M O N   J .   O R T I Z

Photo: Marlene Foster

Beyond and Not beyond Ácoma

Simon J. Ortiz, poet, short fiction writer, essayist, editor, and, lately, a documentary film writer, is a native of Ácoma Pueblo. Ortiz's work includes several collections of poetry, three of which, *Going for the Rain, A Good Journey,* and *Fight Back: For the Sake of the People, For the Sake of the Land,* are reissued in the volume *Woven Stone* (University of Arizona Press, 1992).

Of his work, he states in *Woven Stone,* "In writing, I was very aware of trying to instill that sense of continuity essential to the poetry and stories, essential to Native American life and outlook. I have often heard Native American elders repeat, 'We must always remember,' referring to grandmothers and grandfathers, heritage, and the past with a sense of something more than memory or remembering at stake.

"When I came across the writings of the Beat Generation,...I was struck as if by revelation. It was 'experience' I noticed, the idea of experience, writing from and about experience, and writing as experience. And the revelation that was brought to light for me was that as an Ácoma person, I also had something important, unique, and special to say.

"As an *Aacqumeh hahtrudzi* and a writer, I believe that being real in a real world is loving and respecting myself. This, I believe, has always been the true and real vision of indigenous people of the Americas: to love, respect, and be responsible to ourselves and others."

A STORY OF HOW A WALL STANDS

At Aacqu, there is a wall
almost 400 years old
which supports hundreds
of tons of dirt and bones—
it's a graveyard built on a
steep incline—and it looks
like it's about to fall down
the incline but will not for
a long time.

My father, who works with stone,
says, "That's just the part you see,
the stones which seem to be
just packed in on the outside,"
and with his hands puts the stone and mud
in place. "Underneath what looks like loose stone,
there is stone woven together."
He ties one hand over the other,
fitting like the bones of his hands
and fingers. "That's what is
holding it together."

"It is built that carefully,"
he says, "the mud mixed
to a certain texture," patiently
"with the fingers," worked
in the palm of his hand. "So that
placed between the stones, they hold
together for a long, long time."

He tells me those things,
the story of them worked
with his fingers, in the palm
of his hands, working the stone
and the mud until they become
the wall that stands a long, long time.

V. B.   P R I C E

Evolution of Metaphor

"I am making poems all the time. I carry drafts in my back pocket wherever I go. Making poems is a way of life; I try to be present and ready....I think of New Mexico as a sacred landscape, and many of my poems in the last decade have been written about the relationship between geography and consciousness, land and mind, geological process and the evolution of metaphor."

V. B. Price is a poet, journalist, teacher, and an environmental and architectural critic who has been living and working in New Mexico since 1958. His two latest books are *A City at the End of the World* (University of New Mexico Press, 1992) and a book of poems, *Chaco Body* (Artspace Press, 1990). Price's other books of poetry include *The Cyclops' Garden* (San Marcos, 1969), *Semblances* (Sunstone Press, 1976), and *Documentaries* (Running Women Press, 1985) with book artist Paula Hocks.

"A relationship exists between all human beings who have surrendered to their spiritual instinct. It is a relationship that bonds us across time and culture, so that the imagination of the present has an intimate proximity with the spiritual and emotional life of the Anasazi, or of Homeric peoples, or of all others who, in awe and reverence, have struggled to give form to things unknown."

Price was a founding editor of *Century* Magazine, city editor for the *New Mexico Independent*, and the editor of *New Mexico* Magazine. He teaches in the University of New Mexico General Honors Program and is an adjunct associate professor in the university's School of Architecture and Planning.

He lives in Albuquerque's North Valley with his wife, painter Rini Price.

FROM CHACO BODY

I. TRANSPARENCY

To imagine is to know
with no reference to the truth,
the truth which is without us
only pure.

We believe and we become.

Canyons, kivas, minds
each contain a space
which is
what has contained it.

Power is in opening
so holy nothing is the way.

The canyon comes to you at dawn,
     as a god comes
     full of prophecy, funereal,
light as gravity with nothing left to pull,
     as the past
     fills you
     as a void would,
                exploding in
     as sun fills an open eye.

Here one wears the place as one would wear a mask,
is asked to join a dance one does not understand,
and does it,
        knows it,
        is it and is not,
in union
       with both doubt and play,
       and what one makes of doing

There is no letter of the land,
no gospel code.
The literal means no more than what has formed it
as an instant means no more than what's behind, ahead.

The place is
everything it is,
in time, in mind,
its emptiness
and the front side of its stories.

Chaco body,
deep breathing breezes through the weeds,
rock face changing faces,
imagination knows
the present as transparency,
deep vanishing,
its mask of instants,
knows
what is
is constantly not there,
a focusing
emerged into itself,
over and over,
layer by layer,
a black hole, looking glass
which holds it all,
its molecular days,
its oceans, corpses, gods,
its depths and surfaces of light,
the weight
of its transparencies, stratigraphies,
its harmonies of scree clack,
clouds of river foam, their floating by,
shorelines lapping,
sharks cruising through the cliffs,
flood gusts, virga, lightning far as dreams,
and water in the ditches,
the sound of bells, of beaks, of rattle flutter,
the wondering
in living skulls
in spirit face
risen from the light beneath
to stand
in moon air, hearing still
vibrations

of other worlds, heart drums
in the round soundings of the night
deep underground
where souls diffuse into their flesh
and imagination waits
as possibility in nerves.

Transfigured here,
to imagine is to wear
the mask of endless once,
the canyon
            uttered on your breath
into the space that covers you
as emptiness is covered, instant by instant,
as dreaming
            hardens into sense
so you can vacate where you are,
filled as a mask is filled
with being that is neither
form nor soul
but possibility
worn inside
so you can play at being where you are,
remote, remorseless,
dancing away, unchanging,
circular, in upheaval, straight ahead.

It is dead,
where future dies,
and all around you
you inside
transparent as the lens of now.
And somewhere in the seeing
you disappear,
mind becomes its space,
and your eyes, themselves,
are openings in time.

FROM CHACO BODY

II. ALREADY GONE

Never freed from now,
I cannot hear them,
                    I can have
                    no memory of their lives.
                    Their voices are behind me
            even though I am
                what they have left behind.
                                As if time
                were whole
                and still behind the lives of those
who cannot hear me now,
                        I am the heir
            of their imagining,
                        and am,
                        myself,
                        no more
                        than what
            cannot be known tomorrow.

In the human now
we know them as ourselves.

It was so
on the walk to La Fajada in the polished heat,
the sun inhaling, holding its breath;
it was so
            when nine
            hundred years
            across the dead sand, scrub, and ants
a clump of grasses whirled and hissed
so violently I felt
the holy panic in myself,
the terror vacancy, adrenal gorging and the dread
to hear
            what must have been

the passing of a god
with no one left there
                    to believe it.

Believe the fossil fin,
the tidepool ripples on the canyon wall.
Believe divinity filling voids.

Our questions are the same,
formed from stories
            we cannot know,
                            stranded in our nows.
        But I say,
        as I read the day,
        that the land has memory,
                            that the past must
                    come to it,
                    that it is
            unconsciousness itself,
that there
we all
        are visitors without guides
                        in the un-
                        recollected memory
            of the world.

We are the heirs of all imagining.

Because the canyon knows the death I am,
I know myself
as carapace,
                as lightning freed,
                long gone in light,
        as myth again
        which is to truth
                    as bodies are to death,
                                    mortal as rock,
                as dreams passing through rock,
alive
        with dying,
                    present
                    by being unrecalled,
                    a fine silt

                    waiting for wind,
                                true
                                as a god
    believed through the grasses.

FROM CHACO MIND

II. THE MUSIC OF TIME

It is all one sea,
one sky,
            to the edge
            of the end.

At Pacific's rim off Malibu,
        sailboats slicing through a sunny fog,
we watched the waters
swallow Chaco up,
and we could see
                    no difference
on the surface of the sea.

And as the waves changed places,
the sea between us
was made of ashes
and the air of days,
                days like drops of rain,
like mist, so many days
one after another
                    endless
                    without beginning.

                    (There is
                    nothing
                    more.
                    There is
                    nothing
                    other.)

On Chaco days
      when shirts are sails,
      and wind works dust like water,
I've seen sharks' teeth, like weeds,
cropping up on sandstone flats, have held in my hand
a slab of fish, rock fins and scales flat as shale.
I've seen the nacre of shells, like angel skin
budding through the surface of the rock.

Before "death
and its questionable past,"
I understood so little.
I thought I put my mother's ashes in Pacific Seas,
      released her to the waves
      and she was gone.

But now, the ocean's sound
is just her breathing,
my mind rising and falling
      with the tide of days
      on Chaco's inner shore;
my father's ashes
and my own with hers
rising up in thunderheads
                    chasing poets off the cliffs
                    with lightning fact
that burns through words
so faith, for once,
      is purified of form.

As ghost clouds
boil across the stone flats
with eons of the moon,
I feel her like a thought
released without a sound,
             and see
no difference
on the surface of the sea.

LEROY QUINTANA

The Old Cuentos

Photo: Elisa Quintana

Leroy Quintana is a native New Mexican. He holds an M.A. in English from New Mexico State University and an M.A. in counseling from Western New Mexico University. He is a licensed marriage and family child counselor and a Viet Nam veteran, Infantry/Airborne.

"I try to write as often as possible, as much as possible. I like to work on the keyboard and clean up as I go—it gives me the feeling of finality—but I currently find myself writing rough drafts in a notebook. Each of our daughters has a car, plus our two, so it seems I'm constantly taking some vehicle for repairs. I also have a seven-year-old son who keeps me busy—so any time that I can find to write is valuable."

Quintana has taught at New Mexico State University, El Paso Community College, the University of New Mexico, San Diego State University, and is currently on the English faculty at San Diego Mesa College. His publications include *Hijo del Pueblo: New Mexico Poems* (Puerto del Sol Press, 1976), *Sangre* (Prima Agua Press, 1981), *Five Poets of Aztlan* (Bilingual Press, 1984), *Interrogations* (Viet Nam Generations/Burning Cities Press, 1992), and *The History of Home* (Bilingual Press, 1993).

"I haven't changed much from that little boy who grew up listening to his grandparents tell, in their grand way, tales of La Llorona, of haunted houses and hidden *tesoro*, of the hanging of Black Jack Ketchum. When I go home, I listen to my mother tell the old *cuentos* of our family history. It seems I find myself with each passing year farther and farther from home. What I miss and what I return for is to reacquaint myself with old places, memories, to listen to the old tales, and possibly some new ones, so that I, in turn, can tell them and retell them in the simplest way I know."

Recipient of numerous awards, including the Before Columbus Foundation American Book Award and a National Endowment for the Arts Creative Writing Fellowship, Quintana recently finished editing an anthology entitled *Paper Dance: Fifty-four Latino Poets* with Victor Hernández Cruz and Virgil Suarez (Persea Books, 1994).

LA OPERA

When Roberto's mother asked
him if he liked la opera
he, of course, said, si
because he truly does,
(particularly Puccini),
and she immediately,
said she did not, that
when la Operah came on
at four with her chisme
she immediately switches
to some other channel.

BLUE

Senaida was describing some material
she planned to buy to make a dress:
it was a beautiful blue, however
not just blue, but blue, blue, blue.

According to her you just can't say
dark blue porque los Mejicanos
describe by repeating.
The more times you say blue,
pues, the bluer it becomes.

POEM FOR GRANDMOTHER

Grandmother, how quickly the days pass, how quickly
Today, in the monotony of day to day, I realized
how long it's been since I stopped to think of you
Such is the fate of women, of grandmothers, I suppose
They tell you the old cuentos, comb your hair,
make tortillas, cook your favorite frijoles with hamhock,
smile softly, call you "mi'jito" and heal you, old herbs,
remedios people here would laugh at
They protect you from the harsh demands of grandfathers
who they think want you to be a man long before you are ready
They make candy on old firewood stoves,
tell you stories of their youth, your history
They give you old arrowheads they found in the hills
long ago and they bathe you, forgive you not only
after they send you down the hill to the old Arab's store
for tacks to repair the linoleum and you fling half the box
away causing flats all over the neighborhood, but always
They send you to school, teach you your prayers, tend
small gardens, grow flowers whose names existed only in Spanish,
flowers whose petals you pluck wondering if the freckled girl
down the hill loves you, loves you not, loves you, loves you
All your summers are filled with butterflies
And they cry when you leave which is often
The days pass, years, grandmothers become ill; they die
Still, it is grandfathers we remember best
The men of my family were born to sweat under the sun,
to swing hammers, pound on anvils, shovel coal, crack whips
on the backs of oxen, swear by the devil; a world of horses,
men who shear sheep, fight and die in wars
Our women are meant to stay home, have children
Their place is the kitchen
I am of course the men of home and they are me
But I am also the one who left and returned
time and again left more often than returned
The one who as a child was enchanted by words
Now it seems they haunt me; a thousand lives

I miss your old stories grandmother
I have a deep and desperate need to tell mine
Perhaps that's all I have of home

And all home will have of me
Grandmother how the days pass; How quickly
the days pass. And the road between here and home
seems longer with each passing, weary year
Longer with each passing weary year
If I am not careful,
and I am not a careful man, soon, and that seems very,
I too will be a stranger there

M A R G A R E T   R A N D A L L

Photo: Colleen McKay

Honoring My Craft

"In Mexico, Cuba, and finally Nicaragua—where I lived from 1961 to 1984—I produced at least thirty books, most of them between eleven at night and two or three in the morning. Often my writing space was the corner of a desk or table that also supported a diaper pail with its strong odor of ammonia."

Born in New York City in 1936, Margaret Randall left this country in her mid-twenties. She worked as a midwife, translated Latin American prose and poetry, and became involved in the women's movement. Throughout her twenty-three years in Latin America, Randall spoke and wrote about women's lives and people's culture.

"As I raised my children and participated in the great social upheavals that characterized those years, the writing was always relegated to a kind of 'overtime.' In the mid-eighties, one of my deepest motivations for returning to the States was an intensifying need to make the writing a more central part of my experience."

Author of more than sixty books, Randall came back to the United States in 1984 and was ordered deported under the "ideological exclusion" clause of the 1952 McCarran-Walter Immigration and Nationality Act. She won her case in August of 1989.

"Today I find that long hours of contemplation, even meditation if you like, is essential to my writing process. These days, the act of putting the words on paper seems to be the end part of the process, rather than the expression of immediacy it was when I was younger."

Randall resides in Albuquerque.

RETABLOS FOR FRIDA*

1.

In Mexico I always visit your house.
I know you remember the blue house in Coyoacan
where your trickster spirit
still rises from every kitchen pot.

I always come back to the butterflies
stunned as your broken body
pinned in their glass case
on the underside of the last bed's canopy.

I stop before the papier-mâché Judas
that guards the entrance to your garden,
twenty-foot monster of betrayal,
his volcanic wall of ash.

2.

Our cities are filled with homeless now—
men lead us into fabricated wars,
prepare to celebrate five centuries of occupation.
But of course you know all this.

I share today's calamity as I stare
at the portraits of Marx, Engels, Lenin, Stalin, Mao
fixed like soldiers at the foot of your bed.
And I smile, amused,
remembering you and Trotsky,
your private calendar in San Angel's secret rooms.

3.

Dreaming, I wonder about the women
who laid down with you.

* Frida Kahlo, Mexican painter, 1907–1954.

I search for the fire that must have seared your hands
when you and Tina hid behind each other's eyes.

Each morning's promise,
         retablo for the day just ended
         or the one exuberantly begun.

I too love people—women—
yet there are moments people, even women
                  wear me out.

4.

Dying, you must have known the risk
of instant explanation: *frail...victim...*
         attempted suicide...
They told such easy stories
of others in your time.

How quickly they bared
         your shriveled leg,
your steel-pierced sex revealed to the world.

But then, how not to die
against so many doctors' orders,
         pills, amputation, lies,
biographers whining down your door?

Frida, what recipe held you fast to life
when the energy to fix your ribboned hair was gone?

5.

Ten years before you went
you dreamt a swirling sunflower
         yellow aura of flames
fanned out from your sudden upright face.

That dream became prophecy.

As your body on its palette slid forward

towards the crematorium's mouth
heat jackknifed muscles and you sat up
eyes open
riding hard into the furnace
that would change your molecules.

6.

Frida, my flesh, too, defies me.
Often it hauls forth
its own memories of great empty holes.

Then I remember Hermenegildo Bustos
painter of portraits
dead in Guanajuato days before your birth.

7.

Ten days before death you marched
(in your wheelchair, a wrinkled scarf
hiding the hair you could no longer braid)
pollen of conquered pain already softening your eyes
but Guatemala raised in your tired fist.

8.

There is always Diego, your *saporana*
green frog child
suckling dry the mother's breast.
He still traces history in our eyes
but knew you were the better painter
called you *fierce Mexican innocent.*

Frida, with you I keep
one last memory of your Diego
eyes bulging through tears
taking out his little sketchbook
and drawing your shimmering skeleton
reaching for the flames.

When he died they did not mix his ashes
as he wished with yours.
Jealous wife and daughters,
anticommunism, fear of flames:
all had their hand in the poor rewrite.
He: carried off to the Circle of Illustrious Ones,
you: settled but restless in your dark clay pot.

9.

Knife wounds, little fountains of blood,
twin spirits joined at your broken spine.
Gemini's double helix
will not reduce to one.

The two Fridas only feign their rest
in the closed circle of your unbreakable life.
Only your pain, your full heart and pain
live on in the blue house
and in my impatient rage.

MIRRORS

This woman, toothless at thirty-eight,
laughs at her sister's parchment gaze,
knows the angry row of curls
nudging her baby's ear
but is oblivious to the camera's claim to her.
She cannot find her face
on the surface of this photograph.
There are no mirrors in her hills.

Mirrors chased through **your** childhood
making you watchful and sad.
By tenth grade they gave back Sears Charm School,
father's unwelcome eyes.
Threat of fingers. The belt.
That thick secret.

Now you avoid them, pronounce relief
at the thought of a world where mirrors aren't.

My own mirror taunts a canyon of mist
where Vogue silhouettes hum off-key melodies.
Food uneaten on the plate.
Melted. Changed. The real body
reflecting that other willowed stance.
Perfect skin. And especially the graceful neck.
How I've longed for the grace of that neck ...

That woman who does not recognize
her image in the photograph—
can we say she has never seen herself?
Where is the mirror
unbruised enough to tell us who we are?

YOUR SCISSORED ROOMS OF MEMORY

Each morning, many times a day
you tell me *Finding a bed is so damned hard.*
This is your bed (I touch its metal rail)
this is always your bed.
And your smile remains a question.

Today you are certain your wife of sixty years
is filing for divorce.
She is seeing that doctor, you explain
and mourn as you tug colliding shards,
jigsaw of words that disappear
through cobwebbed doors.

Where are the chambers of connection
in a brain gone stale trying
to find a bed?
Your walls too fragile now
to distinguish infidelities forty years gone cold
from one missed visit.

No divorce, Daddy. No young doctor.
Mother is still your wife.
She'll be here any minute.
This is such a wonderful shock, you say,
I'm filled with joy.
Pathways clear, connections stand
briefly.

Still, I long to take a broom
to your scissored rooms of memory,
sweep them to an easier logic,
pull down the shades
and wail a child's goodnight.

DANCING WITH THE DOE

Each time I relearn dignity one tawny deer
stops tall, then leaps and poses motionless
at the edge of this meadow
darkened by its loss of day.
Bruising the hearty muscle in my breast
it fades to the forest I cannot enter from my fear.

Some days she is fawn, large head
on her perfect body
and soft white spots.
Then she is doe
running with other does,
or the image of one thunderous buck
charging the waters that reshape this land,
its furious grace.

Someone tells a slender friend
she has lost weight
and the friend says *thank you*.
Buck or fawn rear silent in my throat.
It is I who am saying *thank you, thank you*,
words drumming beneath my skin.
And we continue to turn the glossy pages,

strut to the piper's tune, a message
whose tiny belts squeeze hourglass waists
on cans of liquid promise.

Today I dance with the doe.
But I am also buck and fawn
slow motion spiraling and powerful arms
dancing myself in place.
In place in history.
In place in time.
Now the forest unfolds to my eyes
that leap through its secrets like stars.

LEO ROMERO

The Ground on Which I Stand

Photo: Janey Washburn

"Writing poetry for me has been a way of giving myself an identity. In a way I see it as having formed the ground on which I stand; it has created a past from where I come, and as such it allows me to move on to the future with confidence of who I am.

"My three books of poetry, *Agua Negra* (Ahsahta Press, 1981), *Celso* (Arte Público Press, 1984), and *Going Home Away Indian* (Ahsahta Press, 1990), are about New Mexico. *Agua Negra* is about a place, a community, in northern New Mexico. *Celso* was originally a character in *Agua Negra*, but I began writing so many poems about him that I decided to make a separate book. And *Going Home Away Indian* is a Hispano's view—a Chicano's view—of Indians, someone whose roots in New Mexico are deep, with some Indian blood, but predominantly of Spanish ancestry, taking a look at the history of Indians at times from the perspective of Indian bars—or bars where there happen to be Indians.

"For many years, I wrote when I got home from work or during weekends. But a dullness creeps into the poetry when the drudgery of a job takes its toll. So after two or three years I have frequently found it necessary to switch jobs so as to try to bring life to my writing. At times it has been successful for a few months, but then the deadening drudgery takes its toll. Somehow I have managed to keep a tenuous spark going, just barely."

Romero's first book of short stories, *Rita and Los Angeles*, is forthcoming (Bilingual/Review Press). His work has recently been anthologized in *After Aztlan: Latino Poets of the Nineties* (David R. Godine Publisher, 1992) and is being published in *Paper Dance: Fifty-four Latino Poets* (Persea Books, 1994). With his wife, the painter Elizabeth Cook, he runs and owns a Santa Fe bookstore, Books and More Books.

Romero resides in Santa Fe.

WEAVING THE RAIN

I smell the first rain of this spring
and leave the door open
I am reminded of a feeling I had yesterday
while looking at a map of New Mexico
I was overcome by a sense of enormous space
and I caught a whiff of a wind
carrying rain, and I felt the grama grass
moving around me, spreading for hundreds
of miles

Outside the wind is weaving the branches
with their sprays of young leaves
and flowers
The wind deftly weaving the rain
into darkness
as the trees wave

WHAT WAS THERE TO DO ON THE PLAINS

1

Drink beer, drive 90 miles per hour
Drive down dirt roads without signs
Crisscrossing New Mexico and Texas
all night, through corn fields
Onion fields, peanut fields
Somewhere during the night
find a large tin building called
La Estrellita, attracting people
from the small towns of west Texas
Bovina, Friona, Hereford, Muleshoe
who worked in the fields and slaughter
houses, to dance to Mexican music
Cumbias, polkas, rancheras
Outside taking a piss on cotton plants
Stars blurry, and sometime after
sunrise driving into a small town

called Earth, getting our bearings
and heading back to Clovis

2

Drive two hundred miles at night
to get back to family, to the mountains
For the weekend, that's what Val
did every Friday night, drank one
to two six-packs on the way
Hardly ever saw another car
but worried a police car would stop him
And then one Tuesday he was so
fed up with work and the plains
that he left that night
He was going to call in sick
the next morning, but somewhere
before San Jon he smashed into
the back of an unlit trailer rig that had
just pulled onto the highway from
a side road

3

Run over turtles day and night
without meaning to, run over
jack rabbits without meaning to
Buy a large turquoise colored belt
and have your name put on it
Marvel at the immense skies
Watch the sun set over the wheat fields
Count telephone poles from Yeso to Vaughn

Drive four hours to Albuquerque
to hear a country music star
Go necking with women who
would like to get married
and never call them up again
Try to remember what planet you're on
Distances so great that only
an astronomer would feel
comfortable with them

MARILYN MONROE INDIAN

Marilyn Monroe Indian
Luscious cactus
fruit lips
Tight sweater
and tight
black pants
She's got a movie star
look about her
Wind blows up
her dress
and everybody looks
Especially the women
What's she got
that we ain't got
they whisper among
each other
White man approves
of such shapely legs
You're going out
on the town
to Manhattan's
and Los Angeles's
fanciest
You couldn't do
any better
than with
Marilyn Monroe Indian
by your side
Beautiful as she is
she can even read
palms
And no one doubts
her acting abilities
anymore
Me, she says modestly
How could all this
fame
come to me
Little girl
who grew up barefoot

on the reservation
By way of explaining her
other Indians say
she belongs
to the long lost
tribe
of albino Indians
out by Zuni
or someplace

DESERT NIGHTS

I would drive out to the desert
in the late afternoon
and watch the large white flowers
of the Datura swirl open
slowly after the sun set
And after it was dark, the coyotes
would encircle me and make
their strange calls

Some nights I would sit on the doorstep
Too hot to be inside the house
And talk to the neighbor
across the gate
as he sat on his doorstep
Every few words, he would interject
the Spanish word for intercourse
That's all he could ever think of
The heat made it worse
He wanted nothing more in life
than to make it with a woman
But the only people who visited him
were his drinking buddies
and his sister, who he said
wanted to get to know me
I would never say anything
thinking of how fat she was

My car was always breaking down
so I couldn't always drive
out to the desert
And when I did, I would worry
about being stranded for the night
It was cool in the desert at night
The stars were very clear
As much as I tried not to
I kept thinking of women
The mountains, their dark
feminine forms
and the womanly moon

My neighbor always had the same story
but he shared his beer so I listened
What he would do if he only had a woman
And from time to time he would remind me
that his sister liked me
and as usual I wouldn't say anything
but reflected on women I had known
who were far, far away

MIRIAM SAGAN

Heiress of the Beats

"I was born in Manhattan, raised in New Jersey, educated in Boston (B.A. Harvard University; M.A. Boston University, in writing), and lived in San Francisco, and in Martha's Vineyard off Cape Cod. When I moved to New Mexico in 1984, I hated it in Santa Fe. I felt like a stranger; I couldn't walk out in the open space but had to follow the train tracks out of Lamy. But after a while, New Mexico ruined me for any place else—the rest of the world felt too flat, too wet, too low. So I stayed.

"By avocation I am a poet, by trade a teacher, by life a mother. My themes are immigration, displacement, and the stories of people who are somehow somewhere they shouldn't be. My grandparents were Jews who left the Ukraine—after that, my family clung to the East Coast. The West was a revelation to me—I felt I had entered America.

"As a writer I'm an internationalist, by tribe a Jew, by gender a woman who likes heroines and will take them where I can find them, by craft a Beat-derived romantic who looks for the orally-based loose line in poetry."

Miriam Sagan's poetry collection is comprised of fifteen books, chapbooks, and cassette tapes. Her poetry books include *Aegean Doorway* (Zephyr Press, 1984), *Acequia Madre: Through the Mother Ditch* (Adastra Press, 1988), *True Body* (Parallax Press, 1991), *Pocahontas Discovers America* (Adastra Press, 1993), and *The Art of Love: New and Selected Poems* (La Alameda, 1994). Other books include her novel *Coastal Lives* (Center Press, 1991) and two books for children on immigration (John Muir Publications). She recently received a Barbara Deming/Money for Women grant to write a poetry cycle on the life of birth control crusader Margaret Sanger.

Miriam lives on Santa Fe's west side with her husband, Robert Winson, a Zen priest, and daughter Isabel.

SHELL IN THE DESERT

Rebecca Salsbury James, 1891–1968

To paint on glass
Female calla lily, rosebud
Live in the mirror's reversal
As if Taos Mountain
Were reflected in the sky
Inverted cone among stars
A woman collects nudes
Painted by men
The melancholy Russian
Paints her with a slash of lipstick
Something is bothering me
Right here, behind my heart
"A walking woman, a waiting woman
A mourning woman, a devout woman
Adobe, cedar posts, old dry wood."
Cadence of earth and water
Milkweed pod on blue
Everything needs a point of reference
Her hands too crippled
For the tiny colcha embroidery stitches
How did the white conch shell
Come to rest beneath the mesa
Figure in black
Follows the narrow path
Lonely house beneath
Dark mountains, home.

HOTEL FLORA

I want to go to Mexico City and be mysterious and sad
I want a one-way ticket and a blank notebook
I want to stay at the Flora Hotel
Cheap, but very clean,
Hotel with an interior courtyard
Poinsettias that are taller than I am

I want to go to Mexico City and be mysterious and sad
Men, and women too, will look at me and ask
Who is that beautiful mysterious woman
And why is she sad?
Every day at five o'clock
I will walk through the Alameda Gardens
Give one American quarter to each of the first three beggars
Watch the man swallow fire
I will go to the lobby with the Diego Rivera mural
Death walking on a Sunday with Mrs. Death
I will order two shots of tequila
I will drink only one
I will lick the back of my hand
Sprinkle salt on it
Lick that off
Like a child who has stayed all day at the beach
I will drink a shot of tequila with a ghost
I want to go to Mexico City with a borrowed suitcase
All my bras will be black and my underpants white
I will wash them by hand in the little sink
Hang them on the balcony to dry slowly
Smelling of diesel fumes
I will build a shrine on my bureau top:
Red plastic comb, two pesos,
Postcard of Frida Kahlo
Sequined Virgin of Guadalupe
Piece of lava, and a key
To a room that is not mine.

PASSOVER

Jews must be everywhere
Even in La Puebla, New Mexico
Where we pass Good Friday pilgrims
Wearing walkmans
Dusty along the highway.
It's shabbos, the two sets of candles
Adorn the tables
Set with sea shells

Seder means: the order
In which things happen
Egypt means: narrows
For plagues we dip our fingers in the wine
Hail kills your tomato plants
You quarrel
With a neighbor about a wall
A friend is unexpectedly in jail
Baby cries in the emergency room
Homeless men sleep in the arroyo
Stumble across Paseo to the liquor store
So drink four cups of wine
It's only the second time this year
Jews must get drunk
And lie down with our shoes off
On comfortable couches
The children are playing in the dusk
My daughter feeds a large white horse
A bunch of golden apples
Desert smells like the sea
Of sand and wind and something else
Clean, and scoured
Miriam's Well
Springs within
Green oasis that must
Reappear within our hearts
Voices singing slightly off-key
This source of water
Follows us
Despite our exile, wandering.

THE LONESOME DEATH OF FEDERICO GARCÍA LORCA

I sweep the floorboards clean
Off Agua Fria onto Don Juan street
I took a wrong turn
Found myself lost in a tinkling neighborhood
Trees hung with a witchery
Of chimes, tin cans, bird feeders, windmills

Clamor in the mild but wintry air
Small dark knot of men
Clotted ominous on the corner
I was the intruder
Walked fast out of the hush of cigarette smoke
Past a barbed wire fence
Bright with laundry
Fuschia shirt, sky blue pants, red vest
Splotched like Jackson Pollock
Across dry earth, blue sky.

At the age of thirty-five I dedicated myself to art
Put the baby in the stroller and went to the bodega
To buy myself one more ambiguously cool
Bottle of orange pop
To drink the sour bubbles down
On the way home
Past someone's small blue gate
Set into the adobe fence
Pale and peeling blue, or almost white
Entrancing somehow, like the inside of a mosque
A whorl, a wheel, a few
Calligraphic flowers.

Allah be with you,
They still say that
In the north hill towns
Full of dogs and dust
A place of hidden Jews
Lost Arabic. Federico García Lorca
The trouble with being dead—
A lack of tobacco and newspapers
A lack of coffee and strangers
Some sadness inside
Kept you from talking about love directly
The dead have no future but dirt
No assumption of going anywhere.

Federico García Lorca
I took your three names into my body
As a child touches snow and then her belly
Trying to eat the world

I bought your book at 179th street
And Broadway, bookstore at the George Washington Bridge
Bus station, Port Authority
With its frightening bathroom
Its frightening sense of frozen motion
I tried to understand your words:
Don't be named Federico
Don't go out for cigarettes
Don't get shot by fascist soldiers
Don't lie about whose mouth you want to kiss.

It's snowing
I drink the foam on the caffé latte
The Berlin wall is down
A core of the salt mine
Shows crystallized tears
From ocean 250 million years gone
My mother wouldn't buy Spanish olives
After Franco
Everything is different now, everything is the same
The whole world says Adios
The whole world speaks Spanish
You haven't been dead very long
But already without a shadow
You've forgotten what you can't remember
No memory of water, nor of wine.

JIM   SAGEL

A Great and Ancient River

"When I drove my backfiring VW bug into northern New Mexico, I immediately knew my driving days were over. I had found my home, the place to plant my chile and grow my poems. This New Mexico, this gentle place with its long and turbulent memories, not only shapes my writing: it is my work."

Jim Sagel is a bilingual writer who has published eleven books of poetry, fiction, and nonfiction. Recent books include *El Santo Queso/The Holy Cheese* (Ediciones del Norte, 1990), *Otra Vez en la Movida/On the Make Again: New and Collected Poems* (West End Press, 1990), and *Dancing to Pay the Light Bill: Essays on New Mexico and the Southwest* (Red Crane Books, 1992). His newest book is *Where the Cinnamon Winds Blow/Donde soplan los vientos de canela* (Red Crane Books, 1993). Sagel won the Premio Casa de las Americas award in Havana, Cuba, in an international Spanish-language literary competition.

"Though I attempt to write in the language I hear in my inner ear, I nearly always 'hear' my poetry in Spanish. This, I think, is because my second language became the language of my heart and, therefore, the language of my poems. Over the last two decades, my most intimate experiences have been in Spanish, and so my most intimate expression in language comes *en español* as well."

Sagel is Director of Arts and Social Sciences at the University of New Mexico at Los Alamos. He is also an adjunct lecturer for the university Graduate Center and a bilingual language consultant for the Mountain States Multifunctional Resource Center at Arizona State University. He has lived in Española, New Mexico, since 1970 with his wife, Teresa Archuleta-Sagel, a weaver of Rio Grande textiles.

"For me, the landscape of New Mexico and the people who dwell in it are one, just as the literary landscape I create overlaps and resonates with the real world I live in along this great and ancient river."

FOR EARACHES

The problem is, our ears are assaulted by so much noise
    we don't want to hear.
But the bigger pain is not hearing
    the words that we need like oxygen
to keep breathing.

For example: I love you.

Whether your ears are stuffed with life's racket
    or on the verge of starving
the result is the same:
an ache that is almost without equal.

The only cure for such an intimate pain
    is sagebrush.

Chew it well until it forms into a ball.
When you put it in your ears you will smell
    the green sigh of the first forest
bursting through the hot rocks.

It's that the ears need to learn
    how to smell again
just as your eyes must remember the forgotten times
    when they knew what it was
to touch.

I am speaking of a baby's eyes
    that in all their transparency
reach for the colors of the tiny universe that surrounds them.

I am speaking of the eyes of the first man
        who traced the mysterious horizons
of his dawning consciousness.

I am, in the end, speaking of the lover
        whose eyes caress
the visible and invisible configuration of his loved one—
        the first love, whenever she may come—
the first time, no matter how old you may be.

Leave the sagebrush in your ears overnight
        even if the night never seems to be over.

When you remove it you will hear
        all the birds you have ignored in your lifetime
singing in the inner ear of your heart.

PARA DOLOR DE LOS OÍDOS

Lo que pasa es que nos llega a los oídos
        mucho ruido que no queremos oír.
Pero el mayor dolor es el de no oír
        las palabras que como el oxígeno
necesitamos para seguir respirando.

Por ejemplo: te quiero.

O que se atiborren los oídos del estrépito de la vida
        o que se queden en ayunas
lo que resulta es igual:
        un dolor que figura entre los más agudos.

Lo único que puede aliviar
        un dolor tan íntimo es el chamiso hediondo.

Máscalo bien hasta que se te haga bola.
Al metértelo en los oídos olerás el suspiro verde
        de la primera selva brotando de las rocas calientes.

Es que los oídos tienen que aprender
        a oler otra vez
lo mismo como tus ojos deben recordar los tiempos olvidados
        cuando sabían lo que era tocar.

Hablo de los ojos del niño
        que transparentes van tentando todos los colores
de su universo pequeño.

Hablo de los ojos del primer hombre
        que palpaban los horizontes pasmosos
de su naciente consciencia.

Hablo, por fin, del enamorado
        cuyos ojos acarician
la configuración visible e invisible de su amada—
        la primera, cuandoquiera que venga—
la primera vez, por viejo que sea uno.

Hay que dejar el chamiso en los oídos hasta la mañana
        aún cuando la mañana no quiera llegar.

Al quitarlo oirás todos los pájaros
        que habrás ignorado en tu vida
cantando en el laberinto de tu corazón.

FOR TOOTHACHES

Teeth
        like lovers
are poor discriminators of pain.

Whether it's a question of extreme cold or excessive passion
        the result is always the same.
It hurts to chew with a mouth that is dying
        for a kiss.

If your nerves have been laid bare
        by the sweetness of love

there are countless remedies you can try.

Make a hot tea out of thistle or coriander
        and hold it in your mouth until it cools.

Pack your throbbing jaw with the crushed leaves
        of the verbena plant
or use a clove which, as everyone knows,
possesses anesthetic properties.

The powdered root of the "herb of the fish"
        may also be applied
or simply go fishing to see if you can forget.

Of course, not a single one of these remedies will work.

If you want to stop the suffering
        the only thing you can do is tear out your teeth.
But be forewarned:
Love's roots remain alive even after the tooth has decayed.

You're better off learning to live
        with such an invincible ache.

PARA DOLOR DE MUELAS

Las muelas
        igual que los enamorados
no saben distinguir entre categorías de dolor.

O sea mucho frío o demasiado fervor
        les da igual.
Siempre sufre uno al mascar con la boca
que se muere por besar.

Si lo dulce del amor te ha puesto
        todos los nervios al descubierto
hay muchos remedios a los cuales puedes acudir.

Haz un té caliente del cardo santo o del cilantro
    y guárdatelo en la boca hasta que se enfríe.

Introduce en la encía pungente hojas machucadas
    de la vervena
o un clavo que, como todo el mundo sabe,
tiene propiedades anestéticas.

También un polvo hecho de la raíz de la yerba del pescador
    se puede aplicar
o vete a pescar a ver si puedes olvidarte de todo.

Claro que ninguno de estos remedios te ayudará.

Lo único que te puede aquietar
    es arrancarte los propios dientes.
Pero sabe esto:
las raíces del amor quedan vivas aún cuando la muela
    haya decaído.

Más vale aprender a vivir con tan insuperable dolor.

R E B E C C A   S E I F E R L E

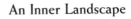

Photo: Phillip Valencia

An Inner Landscape

"Living in New Mexico has been very important to my work. From the beginning of my stay here, I felt that the landscape, dotted with the ruins of a preconquest civilization, its geology in which stark and arid hills still retain the features and fossilized shells of ancient seas, its beauty which exists in a distance that is impossible to inhabit, its otherness, of language, of cultures, of peoples, its sacredness corresponded to my internal landscape."

Rebecca Seiferle lives with her husband and three children in Farmington, New Mexico. She was born in Denver, Colorado, in 1951. Since 1970, she has lived in the Four Corners area of New Mexico. She has been a member of the New Mexico Artists-in-the-Schools program, a librarian, and substitute teacher at Navajo Academy. She is currently an English instructor at San Juan College.

"As the Russian poet Marina Tsvetaeva wrote, poets with history discover themselves 'through the World,' and living in New Mexico has been such an occasion for me. I began writing when I was just fourteen but feel that my first 'real' work began here, some fifteen years ago, when I became engaged with other presences, the presence of my husband and children, the presence of the landscape in which we lived a very rigorous rural life—hauling water, generating our own electricity, raising goats—an otherness which in my previous, intense but ungrounded, preoccupations with history, with languages, with rootlessness and absence, took on a concrete and ordinary dailiness."

Rebecca holds an M.F.A. from Warren Wilson College. Her first collection of poems was *The Ripped-Out Seam* (The Sheep Meadow Press, 1993), and she did a translation of César Vallejo's *Trilce* (The Sheep Meadow Press, 1992). She has won the Bogin Award from the Poetry Society of America, the Writers' Exchange Award, and the Santa Cruz Writers' Union Award.

THE NEW WORLD

As we walk through this arroyo, my daughter,
six, almost seven, years old, kicks up
the handle of a clay pot,
six or seven centuries old. Her fingers
fit the indentation of other fingers,
imprinted in the slight tear at the lip,
and she marvels at that pattern,
tiny waves scalloped
into a curvature.

Look, she says, repeating herself
and retracing the design
because of her happiness at finding it;
here, at the cusp of this hill
where long ago, it must have been used
to drink from a river
that stopped. The earth
is gravid with these black and white shards,
some inscribed with water bugs,
turtles or herons, others scored
by a haphazard geometry.

Each spring, the farmers plow up these ruins,
ruins that Henry James
said didn't exist in America,
but whose relics, nevertheless,
break the harrows of their tractors.
Because this is the first shard
she has ever found, my daughter wants
to keep looking for the whole
that the fragment fits into.

But beneath the roots of the sagebrush
where the rains have hollowed out,
we find only what we are used to finding:
the chamisa's yellow pollen,
the collected sandhills of the ants,
and, most of all, dust, the colorless ground.
Whatever it was, this vessel,
whatever it carried, is broken.

We will never unearth the whole of it,
and yet what my daughter carries home
is enough to disturb everything.

GUATEMALAN WORRY DOLLS

$2.00 with 25% off for liquidation
buys the entire family; their tiny limbs
cropped to fit the space between them,
six of them squeeze into one
thumb-sized house, plaited of straw
like that house in fairy tales
that no one is safe in,
and which they have dyed, knowingly,
with the colors of their fear:
crimson doorways, blue-as-corpse shutters,
piss yellow steps.

One boy smiles without eyes
while a bare wire pokes through the cuff
of his pants, and some of the girls—
or are they women?—have no legs at all
beneath their skirts. Their hair,
just their native soil
glued to the top of their skulls,
rubs off easily, for what welds them together
is some paste of corn and spit.

Ordinary as the laboring days of the week,
the six of them are always searching
for the seventh, the one who disappears
while talking of miracles and peace.
For them, there is no rest; each night,
a child confesses her worries
to each one before burying them all
beneath her pillow, as if they
with their missing eyes and fingers
could bridge the swollen rivers, harvest
the life-sized fields, bake a sugared maize cake,

or, perhaps, *Madre Dios*, empty the machineguns
of the soldiers who have fallen asleep.

It must be true—these tiny figures
must travel, must scuff their shoes
on some road, for they bear the same scars
as those who made them: the red hair of pellagra,
the bellies distended with worms, the appendages
blackened by the National Guard—and, there, beneath
the imperfectly sutured halves of the body—
the fractured, splitting, seam.

RETURNING HOME

Because I have been gone a long time,
I want to buy Maria a present,
and she has seen the kachina dolls gesturing
in the shop windows, among the turquoise God's eyes
and the flat-tasting cactus candy and has been drawn
over and over again to the white and black
severity of this wolf figure, his knees
flexed in the first step of a dance.
Tapping the glass, she points
with the same insistence
with which, at home, she runs
to watch a thunderstorm gather, how
a single flash of lightning floods
a canyon with countless white waves.

The Southwest is full of these wooden
representations; in the churches, each
hand-carved and brightly painted *santo* is
nailed into his niche, as if, otherwise,
he might come down dancing,
and Christ in the rigor of his cross
twists with the sweet-smelling tenacity
of the cedar limbs out of which his own form
was carved. Not stone, not granite, but figures
root-like, vegetable, green

and growing. I, too, have been drawn
to the kachinas, to the owl
opening the snow
sweep of its wings, there, in the dense thicket
of a curio shelf, its gaze like a door,
impossible to close.

But I did not expect my daughter, so young,
to admire this violent gesture of
becoming or to lift this weight,
so willingly, into her hands.
For, yes, it is the wolf she wants, shrouded
in the white skin of what
it has killed: rabbit fur masking its own
slavering jaw. Perhaps the whitewashed
limbs attract her, or the torso painted
with a black cloud where the raindrops
are still falling, or the implied
human form or action, for
when she takes it in her hands, she holds it
to her face like a mask she could inhabit,
or a figure she could follow
dancing through the smallest rooms.

How can I explain to her
that human sacrifice is always disguised like this,
as an animal or a god? For it is said
that before the kachinas were gods,
they were children drowned by the tribe,
and later to console their parents
they returned, but so changed—rattling,
mud-daubed, obscene—they could reveal everything
but their own faces. For it was never
the children themselves—silenced
first in the sacred lake,
then in the myth's retelling—that shuffled
their way out of the kiva, but others,
moved by pity, to restore what had been lost.

But it is out of happiness that Maria
wants this figure, and when it nestles
in a box beneath her arm, she takes my hand

and begins telling me a story,
how when we reach home, our house will be
full of kachinas. Everywhere
on the floors, in the beds, in the cupboards,
a hundred, no, a thousand kachinas,
dancing and singing because, yes,
we have come back.

JOSEPH SOMOZA

In the Backyard

Joseph Somoza is an immigrant who came to the United States from Spain at eight years of age. His first encounters with the States were Elizabeth, New Jersey, and Chicago. He has taught at New Mexico State University in Las Cruces for the past twenty years and has been poetry editor of *Puerto del Sol* for twelve years.

"I like to sit in my backyard in Las Cruces to write. I usually bring a book of poems by someone whose language I find intriguing and flip through it until something in the language grabs me. Sometimes this will lead to a bit of language of my own that might lead into a poem. What I like best about poetry writing is freedom and discovery.

"Living in New Mexico for the past twenty years has shaped who I am. It has relaxed me and brought me more in tune with the small, everyday things around me. I like to observe animals, birds, trees, flowers that are sharing a particular moment of life with me in the yard. This fascinates me more than political or even most social realities ... I see poetry as a way of thinking."

Joseph Somoza has published four books of poetry, the most recent is *Out of This World* (Cinco Puntos Press, 1990). He has given over a hundred poetry readings throughout the Southwest and elsewhere. He lives in Las Cruces with his wife Jill, a painter, and their three children.

PRECIOUS

One cat is sleeping
on the slipper on my foot, while
the other cat
went somewhere.
You can't tell where.
It's so much autumn
now, the leaves are broad-
cast on the lawn.
The lawnchairs. Hardly any
on the tree.
The boughs don't shade
much. Not much
shade needed, though.
Which is just fine. Just
sitting. Whistle
of a train climbs up
from down below
through air fine
as a precious gem
you couldn't find
fault with.

INCARNATION

Now that we're back,
come over. Overcome,
in other words, like the plum tree
looking green and well
despite its torn bark.
One wonders
where the sap goes, how
it rises. It must be
an "unsolved mystery"
like reincarnation, or the original
carnation
that I carried damp to her house
wanting to please her parents

with a scent of pink,
a blush, so to speak,
to start things.
And then out the door
to happily ever after,
or so we thought, perspiring
under our bright clothes,
brighter expectations, brightest
of the graduating class, most
popular and special and good and certain
to succeed. Not
that I'm calling up
the snows of yesteryear, heaven forbid.
In fact, the stream is rushing
in torrents over largish
rocks, causing passersby
to notice. Even the tourist
from Ohio, drawn mostly
by news of Indian jewelry
in the plaza.
But situated on this bridge
between now and formerly,
we can watch the pristine light
reflecting on the current,
never the same current twice,
which is healthier
for you (except, of course,
if there's a cow
decaying upstream). So
come over!
We can review
the albums—though, really,
life is still ahead,
clicking her high heels
into a doorway, swishing
her skirt-suit from the '30s,
hat at a seductive angle,
exhaling from her Philip Morris,
completely bored
by what you or I would consider
"the thing to do"
or "the way to be."

ARTHUR SZE

Translations Character by Character

Arthur Sze has published five books of poems: *Archipelago* (forthcoming from Copper Canyon Press), *River River* (Lost Roads Publishers, 1987), *Dazzled* (Floating Island Publications, 1982), *Two Ravens* (Tooth of Time Books, 1984), and *The Willow Wind* (Tooth of Time Books, 1981). Two books, *The Willow Wind* and *Two Ravens*, contain translations of classical Chinese poetry—Li Po, Wang Wei, T'ao Ch'ien, Ma Chih-yuan, Wen I-to, as well as Sze's original work. He is the recipient of a George A. and Eliza Gardner Howard Foundation Fellowship, two National Endowment for the Arts Creative Writing Fellowships, two Witter Bynner Foundation for Poetry Fellowships, a New Mexico Arts Division Interdisciplinary Grant, and the Eisner Prize, University of California at Berkeley.

"The translations were valuable for me to do because I had to struggle, character by character, through the Chinese poems. Now I am working primarily in sequences. A sequence allows me the flexibility to shift direction, rhythm, energy, without being tied to an overt linear line."

Sze lives with his family in Santa Fe and is currently Director of the Creative Writing Program at the Institute of American Indian Arts.

THE FLOWER PATH

Down to this north end of the verandah, across the view
of 1,001 gold-leafed statues of Kuan-yin looking west,
Wasa Daihachiro, in twenty-four hours in 1686, shot
13,054 arrows of which 8,133 were bull's-eyes. Today
no one can pull the two hundred pound laminated bamboo bow
to send a single arrow with a low trajectory the length
of the thirty-three bays. As you walk on the verandah,
you see a tree full of white bags tied over peaches,
hear the sound of bells at a fish auction,
note the stares of men sitting in tiers under lights;
you are careful not to raise your hand as you examine
a two hundred pound tuna smoking just unpacked from dry ice;
at lunch you put a shrimp in your mouth and feel it twitch;
you enter a house and are dazed as your eyes adjust to
a hundred blind Darumas in the room;
you must learn to see a pond in the shape of the character "mind,"
walk through a garden and see it from your ankles;
a family living behind a flower arrangement shop
presents the store as a face to the street;
the eldest daughter wince when the eighty-year-old parents
get out wedding pictures of the second daughter;
at night the belching sounds of frogs;
in the morning you look in rice paddies and find only tadpoles;
you are walking down into a gorge along the river,
turn to find stone piled on stone offerings along the path
and on rocks in mid-stream; in the depths of the cave,
a gold mirror with candles burning;
deer running at dusk in a dry moat;
iris blooming and about to bloom;
you are walking across Moon-Crossing Bridge in slashing rain,
meet a Rinzai monk with a fax machine
who likes to crank up a victrola with a gold horn;
you see the red ocher upper walls of a tea house,
and below the slatted bamboo fences called "dog repellers";
you stop at the south end of the verandah and look north;
an actor walks off the flower path ramp cross-eyed amid shouts.

ORIGINAL MEMORY

1
White orchids along the window—
she notices something has nibbled the eggplant leaves,

mantises have not yet hatched from the egg.
"*Traduttori, traditori*," said a multilinguist

discussing the intricacies of Hopi time and space,
but the inadvertent resonance in the mind

is that passion is original memory:
she is at the window pointing to Sagittarius,

she is slicing *porcini* and laying them in a pan,
she is repotting a cereus wearing chalcedony and gold earrings,

she is judging kachinas and selecting the simplest
to the consternation of museum employees.

Grilled shrimp in olive oil—
a red sensation pours into his thought and touch:

the sfumato of her face,
shining black hair reaching down to her waist;

he knows without looking the plum
bruises on her thigh from the spikes of a sectional warp.

2
The multilinguist wants to reveal the locations
of shrines on the salt trail in the Grand Canyon

but has been declared persona non grata by the tribe.
He may have disproved the thesis that the Hopi language

has no referents to time, but his obsession led
to angers and accusations, betrayals and *pentimenti*:

a cry of a nuthatch vanishes into aquamarine air.
Some things you have to see by making a pinhole,

holding a white sheet of paper at the proper focal length?
To try to retrace the arc of a passion is to

try to dream in slow motion a bursting into flame?
You are collecting budding yellow tea plants;

I am feeling a sexual splendor in a new orchid leaf.
What is the skin of the mind?

How do you distinguish "truth" from "true perception"?
When is an apex a nadir and a nadir an opening into a first world?

Italians slice *porcini*, lay them on screens in the sun,
let the maggots wriggle out and drop to the ground.

3
She is tipping water out of a cloud.
By candlelight, face-to-face,

the pleasures of existence are caught in a string of pearls.
He remembers her rhythm in a corn dance,

notices the swelling of her left ear from a new earring.
He does not want any distortion—

red leaves falling or beginning to fall,
bright yellow chamisa budding along a dirt road,

snow accumulating on black branches—
to this moment of chiaroscuro in which their lives are a sphere.

Face-to-face, by candlelight,
the rock work and doorways form a series of triptychs.

She remembers hiking the trail up to Peñasco Blanco,
sees the Chuska Mountains violet in the west,

and, below, the swerve of Chaco Wash,
the canyon opening up: ruins of rock walls

calcined in the heat, and, in red light,
swallows gathering and daubing mud along the cliff face.

WHITEOUT

You expect to see swirling chunks of ice
flowing south toward open water of the ocean,
but, no, a moment of whiteout as you
see the swirling ice flow north at sunset.
In a restaurant with an empty screen,
a woman gets up and sings a Chinese song
with "empty orchestra" accompaniment.
Prerecorded music fills the room,
and projection from a laser disc throws
a waterfall and red hibiscus onto the screen.
You are not interested in singing and
following the words as they change color
from yellow to purple across the cueing machine.
Instead, you walk out on blue-green glacier
ice and feel it thin to water in spring.
You notice two moose along the thawing shoreline
browsing for buds, and see the posted sign
"No shooting from here." But "here" is "there."

FROM THE ROOFTOP

He wakes up to the noise of ravens in the spruce trees.
For a second, in the mind, the parsley is already
bolting in the heat, but then he realizes
the mind focusing rays into a burning point of light
can also relax its intensity, and then
he feels the slow wave of the day.

Mullein growing by the gas meter
is as significant as the portulaca blooming in pots.
Ants are marching up the vine onto the stucco wall
and into the roof. From the rooftop,
he contemplates the pattern of lightning to the west,
feels a nine-pointed buck edge closer to the road at dusk,
weighs a leaf and wonders what is significant,
maybe the neighbor who plays the saxophone
at odd hours, loudly and badly, but with such expanse.

ANNE VALLEY-FOX

Photo: Anna Christine Hansen

I Require Darkness to Begin

"When I first visited New Mexico, in the early 1970s, I hitchhiked up from El Paso. That summer I helped my sister's family build a house. In the late afternoons we would thread down a trail into the Rio Grande Gorge, carrying the smallest children on our backs and shoulders, and swim in the river. The following summer I moved to New Mexico for good. Choosing to live here, my personal writing process reflects this landscape. I generally require darkness, or early light, and vast stretches of open space, to begin. I begin with an image or a musical line, dive in, establish a stroke, and with luck emerge someplace strange and strangely familiar."

Anne Valley-Fox was born in New Jersey, raised in Pennsylvania, Ohio, and California, and educated at the University of California, Berkeley (1964 to 1968). She is the author of a book of poems, *Sending the Body Out* (Zephyr Press, 1986). With coauthor Sam Keen she published *Telling Your Story* (Doubleday & Company, 1971), which was reissued as *Your Mythic Journey: Finding Meaning in Your Life through Writing and Storytelling* (Jeremy P. Tarcher, 1989). An audio cassette, read by the authors, was released by Bantam Books in 1992.

"Santa Fe is my home. I moved to northern New Mexico with my one-year-old son Ezra in 1977. For seven years now, I've lived with my partner and our combined sons, including our new one, Kalu Browning Long. I am currently writing a prose work with the working title of *Stepmother*.

"I swim in and out of writing poetry and prose—the one provokes the other. Form evolves from content and from interior weather. When I sense a storm front moving in, I'm interested—eager for wind, drizzle, hail, snow flurry, shadow, or garrulous downpour."

GREEN TARA

Seagrass, eyes
in the feathers of peacocks, Tara's green arms
like Medusa's hair, she speaks
in me, cool and green, passing her image pasted on
the refrigerator: *Make a wish!*
At last I screw up last-ditch courage
wrung from ancient sorrows, and say: *Send me love.*

Green Tara, she doesn't mess around.
Next thing I know I am big with child.
I had, of course, envisioned something
other—rollercoaster
with stained seats, White Horse Scotch
downed by the sea and dark sex
to blind me.
But Tara, she has a raucous
sense of humor. The day she sends me a son
she appears with headlights
blinking in her
hair: *G.T. delivers the goods!*

A decade later she sends
more goods, a man
in a green sweater. His love is like a river of
lotus, complex patterns without
complication. Between us the world is overrun
with children. Heedlessly
they trample municipal gardens, we stand them in corners
suppressing giggles, chagrinned
in embrace.

We have not said aloud to each other: *Our blood
grows incessantly greener.*

WAKING

In sleep there are stairs   knives   sirens
you can't help this   you roll in your shell
in the sea   Your dreams congeal like gumtrees
and smoke   blotching the blue   Frightened
you go to the devil's bed and let him undo
your buttons   He tells you he has been mis-
understood   his kisses blister   you long for
obliteration

Without waking you've moved into town   rented
a room   enrolled in Jewelry and Basic Computer
The government sends you compensation   you
drink with friends who feed your despair with
fiendish laughter—one thing leads to another
Climbing the stairs you ask how much higher—
you no longer care where you're going

If you would wake   Aurora whispers   *something
must be returned to the night*   Mounting
the steps you receive the knives and sirens into
your body   turning back fear   your protective
blindness   You wake to a subtle change in the
weather   Something is needing you here: lay
a fire   wash a pot   put something in it   and late
in the day you may pause to feel the gathering
darkness   Evening travels under your skin   wind
blowing through stellar cells between
your tissues you sleep from now on with
riverbed stones weighting your eyelids   Lifting
them carefully off at dawn you practice
waking empty

THE WHEEL

Desiring to wrap them
around you, *"Oh, that I had arms and legs
in multiples like Shiva!"*—

laugh, take it
back, it is wanton to envy the gods
when already we are
flushed with them

You say you are washed, the sands, each cove in
the body cleansed by every
breath—
on a darker day
we go out in the rain
and stand with our faces
gasping into the sky

THE CONTINENTAL DIVIDE
(For Ezra and Aaron, surviving a car wreck)

A clerk at the Stop N' Go in Bernalillo
hands me a fresh carnation
for Mothers Day—crimped crimson
nods at me from a plastic cup wedged among blocks of
firewood on the front seat. Wind is rocking

popcorn clouds driving north
towards Pueblo Bonito, and off of an old recording T. S. Eliot's
heartbroken voice is crackling
The Waste Land. This morning I dreamed

a pilot was killed, alone
in a grounded plane; a woman and slumbering infant escaped
by the skin of their teeth. Pressed to my husband's chest at dawn
he saw himself as the man in flames and me
as survivor, safe in my bond with

the children. And yet I am fleeing … driving north
and west towards beauty, alone and intent
on reaching a spot where prayers of spirits who lived in the earth
strike the air like tongueless bells
to console me: Our children, our teenage

beauties are bleeding—the wasteland
swallows them, spits them out, they are slashed
by desire to jet to the stars
and pluck them. My own desires have flown out the windows
or drag the bottoms of rivers. I contemplate

shucking the weights of the body—but no
such luck! They need us for fuel. They need us for truth.
They need our faces, glinting like sieves in the afternoon
shadows to turn and see
through them.

Crossing the Continental Divide I am cruising under
Apache sky, gulping twisted
winds. On impulse
I veer up a mountain road, red cliffs in the rear-view
mirror glinting metallic

light. Around a curve beside a trailer
some kids are playing ball. A tall girl makes a basket.
Someone has painted and posted a sign: *Slow—Children Playing!*
I glide to a stop—*slow! slow!*—my prayers climbing the blue
air for those shimmering mirrors, those shattering beings
we love to call our children.

KEITH WILSON

I Was Born on This Land

Keith Wilson is a native New Mexican. He is a graduate of the United States Naval Academy (B.S.) and the University of New Mexico (M.A., a.b.d.). He is a former poet-in-residence and professor emeritus at New Mexico State University. He has published more than twenty books of poetry, including *Lion's Gate: Selected Poems 1963–1986* (Cinco Puntos Press, 1988) and *Graves Registry* (Clark City Press, 1992). His poems have been translated into Spanish, Hungarian, Polish, Japanese, German, Rumanian, and Indonesian, and his work has been widely anthologized.

"I was born on this land and, God willing, I will die on it. Everything here has shaped me and, consequently, my poetry, my stories, my teaching, my loves. My two languages, English and Spanish, have formed my throat and filter what I see and hear.

"My compulsion is of New Mexico, of this land itself and its temporary peoples. My allegiance is first to the land, to the kachinas and holy Mother Earth who have guarded it all for so many million years. I feel the telescoping corridors of the centuries always closing about me. *Now* is such a long time. I really write about all that, not New Mexico."

In 1988, Keith received the Governor's Award for Excellence in the Arts. He has also been a D. H. Lawrence Fellow and a Fulbright-Hayes Professor in Rumania. He has been nominated twice for the National Book Award and received a National Endowment for the Arts Creative Writing Fellowship.

"We in New Mexico still have a 'region.' We are perhaps the last heartbeat of the old ways, the old religions. When so many people now live in the greyness of cities, we out here seem strange. I don't view that as a loss, though."

Wilson lives in Las Cruces.

I have learned to wait until
the excitement of the eye sinks
down and allows the mind and the
feelings to function. When feeling
begins, awareness grows. It is then
I begin to paint, the forms become
clear, so do the colors and the inner
life of the people and the place. I
feel that I have then touched the
hidden core.

—Dorothy Brett
"Painting Indians"
To her, her memory

Near the center, the pain
quietly loses its sense as pigment
becomes flesh—the dancing muscles
jerking taut, flecks of dust
spot the firm skin.

From the real drum
                    beats sound out
beyond the paintpot. Color fires more
than a construct of time. Hear. Out
of time, ritual brings all to a point:

        the finished object rising, a bubble
        complete within an undisturbed mine
        perfectly contemplating the whole.

        the dancer always dwells within

Ritual, a rhythm inextricable from the heart's
quick song, the deep singing inside.

RIVER GIRL
—for my wife Heloise

> *more precious is the touch*
> *of your mouth in the shadow*
> *—Jorge Luis Borges*

and I remember the shade
of cottonwoods, the deepgreen solitude.
Cedar breaks, with wind.

How you never stood beside me
there, where shadows became dreams:
sunlight, a confusion, a breaking of mirrors.

Wherever we are now, in the turnings
of nightmare, our worlds speeding us on
to separate destinies (though together)

we still walk that whispering River back
to our young faces enshrouded by trees, and green.
I have always held your eyes.
You cannot have them back now.

PORTRAIT
—for Avelino Borunda

He is no longer with us, my neighbor
who cared for my children, laid in bed
with them when we rushed Kerrin
to the hospital with double pneumonia.

Avelino spoke to me every morning
in English, I responded in Spanish.
Five years later, when I was leaving
the village he forgot and spoke his tongue.

I replied and he said, "Keith!
You speak Spanish!" with such astonishment
such pleasure that his Anglo friend
could say some of the old words.

At least I could give him that,
that gentle man with his dogs
and cats and chickens and family
always about him. Avelino.

"¿Qué tal, Avelino?" "¡Bien,
siempre bien, amigo!"
He lies near San Miguel
where he has always lived.

Most of the village mourns him
as do I and my whole family.
Lights are on in his house tonight
but the doorway misses his shadow.

THE ENCIRCLED GROVE

> *I never understand anything*
> *until I have written about it.*
> —Horace Walpole

And written here is the ceremony of the land
itself, without commentary, other than what it,
this grove, places before the senses. In the deep cool
of glades, clumps of twisted salt cedar, snake-
barked cottonwoods with trunks twice as thick
as a man, broad leaves pushing at the sunlight
that only glimmers down to the moist earth
with its beetles and ferns.

The grove is circular out of ancient incantation,
some enchantment older than Comanche spoke here,
formed this protected world and held it against
wind or geology. The high plain stops at the edge

of its greenness, swirls around it, continues
as far as the eye travels the spreading land
and domed blue hold it in their rushing powers.
Sky Father. Earth Mother. Here is the point
equidistant, focused, the navel that magic flows
through

                    As I passed through
shaped, protected, set free by the Pecos River
and the wind from the quarrels of family, whispers
that held our old house fast. Grandmother's ghost
could never walk in the Bosque where silence became
a moistness, held your breath like another pair
of murmuring lips

                              —*for my brother, Simon Ortiz*

ROGER ZELAZNY

Love at First Sight

"My living in Santa Fe, New Mexico, is a result of a search I'd begun in the early 1970s for a congenial place to live and work. We moved here in January of 1975 and still live in the same, though much-augmented, home. The reason for this instance of love at first sight was that the town met almost all of our needs. It felt like a good place to raise kids. After a while, bits of New Mexico began finding their way into my stories."

Roger Zelazny is the author of over fifty books of science fiction, including *Lord of Light* (Mercury Press, Inc., 1967), *Eye of Cat* (Avon Books, 1991), and *A Night in the Lonesome October* (William Morrow & Company, 1993). His work has been translated into French, Spanish, Portuguese, Italian, German, Dutch, Swedish, Greek, Polish, Russian, Bulgarian, Serbo-Croatian, Hebrew, Japanese, and Chinese. He has won The Science Fiction Achievement Award (Hugo) six times and The Science Fiction Writers of America Nebula Award three times.

"I became fascinated by this corner of the world. I had grown interested in the Navajos—without any intention of using Navajo materials in fiction, I might add—but the more I learned of them, the more I felt a story coming into being. Then one day the idea for a book was there, and I wrote it. It was called *Eye of Cat*, and it occupies a special place in the house of my memory called Favorite Things I Have Done."

Zelazny lives with his wife, Judith Alene Callahan, and their three children in Santa Fe, New Mexico.

WALKING, OF COURSE

Walking, of course, away from it all,
the run and the crawl.
Walking as we must
beyond tales end, the dark,
the light, and the grey, past
reefs of bleached buffalo bone,
the seasons, the years,
the opened graves and closed,
the burnt villages and blackened plain
where time the river flows,
we look for real endings, finding none,
and graves that come and go.

John Colter died leaving

> *2 beds, 4 chairs, one glass tumbler,*
> *1 dish and 5 puter plates,*
> *1 plow, 1 hoe, one Dutch oven,*
> *2 pie pans, 3 puter basins,*
> *1 coffee pot, 1 little spinning wheel,*
> *2 bottles, 4 tin cups,*
> *knives, forks and spoons,*
> *1 piggin, 1 pane of cotton cards,*
> *1 flat iron, 3 books,*
> *1 mare, 1 colt, one heffer,*
> *1 cow and calf.*

His estate, settled December 10, 1813,
was valued at $233.76–3/4
after his debts had been paid,
and, in an unmarked grave on Tunnel Hill,
outside St. Louis was he laid, later forgotten,
and used as landfill,
becoming part of the track bed
of the Missouri Pacific Railway.

None knows where Old Hugh
came to rest, though Jamie Bridger'd
a Wyoming fort to bear his name.

Walking then away from it all
down endless caverns,
through citied futures,
one finds, as at the end of every trail,
a skull. Whose, is hardly important,
but that into the coming together place
where time crosses the world, it held
the act of continual passion,
granting meaning to the bright moment
of its execution, beneath sun, sky, stars,
where lives and futures fuse,
turning courses away from the greater darkness,
signing the earth with the long pressure of its gaze.

Walking, you see them painted now
in ancient halls of the Earth;
walking, you see them all painted,
deep, on the walls of the cave.

CREDITS

LUCILE ADLER

"At the Cave Mouth" is from *The Society of Anna*, The Lightning Tree, Santa Fe, New Mexico, 1974. "after the seige of Leningrad" is from the manuscript The Red Pear Tree, 1993. "The Mesa We Climbed" is from the manuscript The Heart Determines, 1993.

MEI-MEI BERSSENBRUGGE

"Chinese Space" is from *Empathy*, Station Hill Press, Barrytown, New York, 1989. It was first published in *Conjunctions Magazine*. "Sphericity" is from *Sphericity*, Kelsey Street Press, Oakland, California, 1993. It was first published in *Grand Street*.

JOHN BRANDI

"I Saw Kit Carson Still Alive" and "This Language Isn't Speech" are from *Shadow Play*, Light and Dust Books, Kenosha, Wisconsin, 1992.

ANA CASTILLO

Quoted excerpts in the biography are reprinted from an interview with Robert Birnbaum, *Stuff Magazine*, June 1993. "You Are Real as Earth, y Mas": Copyright © 1991 by Ana Castillo, first published in *Berkeley Poetry Review*, vol. 25, 1991–1992. "You First": Copyright ©1990 by Ana Castillo, first published in *Bombay Gin*, Naropa Institute, Summer 1990. "The Road to Zacapo": Copyright ©1992 by Ana Castillo, first published in *Puerto del Sol*, vol. 27, no.1, 1992. Reprinted by permission of Susan Bergholz Literary Services, New York.

DENISE CHÁVEZ

"Artery of Land": Copyright © 1988 by Denise Chávez. First published in *Chicana Creativity and Criticism: Charting New Frontiers in American Literature*, edited by María Herrera-Sobek and Helena María Viramontes, Arte Público Press, 1988. "Mercado Day" and "Legaña of Lace": Copyright © 1987 by Denise Chávez. First published in *The Americas Review*, vol. 15, no. 1, Spring 1987. Reprinted by permission of Susan Bergholz Literary Services, New York.

JUDSON CREWS

"I am still as stone" and "Returning to Taos, after many seasons" appeared in *Clock of Moss*, Ahsahta Press, 1983.

VICTOR DI SUVERO

"To Live with the Beloved" and "Winter Solstice" are from *Tesuque Poems*, The Pennywhistle Press, Tesuque, New Mexico, 1993.

MARTIN EDMUNDS

"The High Road to Taos": Copyright © 1994 by the Board of Trustees of the University of Illinois, Urbana-Champaign and Chicago, Illinois. Used with permission of the University of Illinois Press. "Taos" and "A Hill Village" were originally published in *Grand Street*, vol. 12, no. 2, Summer 1993. "The Morada. La Muerte" was published in the *New Yorker*.

GENE FRUMKIN

"White Panther" was printed in *New Mexico* Magazine, vol. 54, no. 9, September 1976; *Voices from the Rio Grande*, anthology published by the Rio Grande Writers Association, first printing

December 1976; *The Mystic Writing-Pad*, The Red Hill Press, Los Angeles, California, 1977; and *Saturn Is Mostly Weather: Selected and Uncollected Poems*, Cinco Puntos Press, El Paso, Texas, 1992. "Saturn Is Mostly Weather" was printed in *Poetry Northwest*, vol. 24, no. 1, Spring 1983; and *Saturn Is Mostly Weather: Selected and Uncollected Poems*, Cinco Puntos Press, El Paso, Texas, 1992. "Stanford Street Poem" was printed in *The Nation*, vol. 207, no. 23, December 30, 1968; *Clouds and Red Earth*, Swallow/Ohio University Press, Athens, Ohio, 1981; *The Rainbow-Walker*, Grasshopper Press, Albuquerque, New Mexico, 1969; and *Saturn Is Mostly Weather: Selected and Uncollected Poems*, Cinco Puntos Press, El Paso, Texas, 1992. "Salmon in the Pool" was published in *Floating Island IV*, Floating Island Publications, Point Reyes Station, California, 1989; and *Saturn Is Mostly Weather: Selected and Uncollected Poems*, Cinco Puntos Press, El Paso, Texas, 1992.

GREG GLAZNER

"Leaving the Vigíl Studio" and "Fin de la Fiesta" were first published in *From the Iron Chair*, W. W. Norton & Company, New York, New York, 1992, and are reprinted with permission of W. W. Norton & Company.

LARRY GOODELL

"The House That Makes It So" was printed in *The Sign Post*, Placitas, New Mexico, August 1993.

RENÉE GREGORIO

"Silent Dialogue" was printed in *Blue Mesa Review*, vol. 3, Spring 1991. "The Final X" was published in *The X Poems*, X Press, Santa Fe, New Mexico, 1992.

JOY HARJO

"The Myth of Blackbirds" and "The Place the Musician Became a Bear" were printed in *The Kenyon Review*, vol. 15, no. 3, Summer 1993.

GERALD HAUSMAN

"Juniper" originally appeared in *Willow Springs*, vol. 15, Winter 1985. "The Old Ways" originally appeared in *The Native American Today*, vol. 6, nos. 1, 2, 1986.

JUDYTH HILL

"Grist for Grace" is reprinted from *Altar of the Ordinary*, Yoo-Hoo Press, Farmington, New Mexico, 1993. "Samurai Angels" is reprinted from *HardWired for Love*, The Pennywhistle Press, Tesuque, New Mexico, 1990.

ELIZABETH SEARLE LAMB

Publication data on the haiku:

almost daybreak	*The Red Pagoda*, Special Edition, April 1985
on the ditch bank	*Brussels Sprout*, vol. 10, no. 1, 1993
a white horse	*Frogpond*, vol. 14, no. 3, Autumn 1991
raised by a hoist	*Modern Haiku*, vol. 22, no. 2, Summer 1991
this morning	*Haiku Southwest*, vol. 1, no. 1, January 1993
the broken harp string	*Casting into a Cloud* (From Here, 1985)
he prunes the juniper	*Casting into a Cloud* (From Here, 1985)
the brown-robed priest	*Modern Haiku*, vol. 18, no. 3, Autumn 1987
autumn's full moon—	*The World Haiku Contest* (Japan) 1989
Española lowriders	*The Red Pagoda*, vol. 3, no. 4, Spring 1986
half silted under	*The Red Pagoda*, vol. 3, no. 4, Spring 1986
far back under a ledge	*Casting into a Cloud* (From Here, 1985)
tossing a stone	*Haiku International* (H.I. Association, Japan, 1992)
a lizard inching	*Casting into a Cloud* (From Here, 1985)
a flight of birds	*Noctiluca*, vol. 1, no. 2, Winter 1993

a candle burns	*Ant Farm*, vol. 3, 1991
a field of wild iris	*Casting into a Cloud* (From Here, 1985)
wind in the sagebrush—	*Casting into a Cloud* (From Here, 1985)
a blue pickup	*Casting into a Cloud* (From Here, 1985)
early blizzard	*Modern Haiku*, vol. 22, no. 1, Winter/Spring, 1991

"Mission Ruins" was previously published in *Studia Mystica*, vol. 7, no. 2, Summer 1984.

DONALD LEVERING

"Weaving Cave—Frijoles Canyon" was previously published in *New Mexico Humanities Review*, Summer 1984.

HAROLD LITTLEBIRD

Quoted excerpts in the biography are reprinted from *Literature and Landscape: Writers of the Southwest* by Cynthia Farah with permission of Texas Western Press, El Paso, Texas, 1988. "In a child's memory" was previously published in *Returning the Gift*, University of Oklahoma Press, Norman, Oklahoma, 1993.

JOAN LOGGHE

"Something Like Marriage" previously appeared in the *Santa Fe Reporter*, 1992, and *Honoring the Muse: Four Santa Fe Poets*, Video Magic, Santa Fe, New Mexico, 1993. "High School Graduation Pantoum" and "Something" are reprinted from *What Makes a Woman Beautiful*, The Pennywhistle Press, Tesuque, New Mexico, 1993.

DEMETRIA MARTINEZ

"Only Say the Word: A Poem for Three Women's Voices" is from a collection of poetry, *Turning*, which appears in an anthology of three Chicana poets titled *Three Times a Woman*, Bilingual Press, Tempe, Arizona, 1989.

MARY McGINNIS

"Desert Stones Talking" was published in the *Utah Wilderness Association Newsletter*, May/June 1991. "Reading Braille" was published in *Womyns Braille Press Newsletter*, Spring 1991, and *Disability Rag*, Advocado Press, Louisville, Kentucky, 1993.

CAROL MOLDAW

"Beads of Rain" was published in *The New Yorker*, November 30, 1992.

NORA NARANJO-MORSE

All poems are reprinted from *Mud Woman: Poems from the Clay*, University of Arizona Press, Tucson, Arizona, 1992.

SIMON J. ORTIZ

"A Story of How a Wall Stands," previously published in *Going for the Rain*, Harper & Row, Inc., New York, 1976, is reprinted by permission of the author.

V. B. PRICE

"Transparency," first published in the Summer 1988 edition of *Artspace*, and "Already Gone," first published in the November 1988 edition of *New Mexico* Magazine, are from *Chaco Body*. "The Music of Time" is from Chaco Mind. Chaco Trilogy contains *Chaco Body*, *Chaco Elegies*, and Chaco Mind.

MARGARET RANDALL

"Retablos for Frida," "Mirrors," and "Dancing with the Doe" were previously published in *Dancing with the Doe*, West End Press, Albuquerque, New Mexico, 1992.

LEO ROMERO

"Weaving the Rain" first appeared in *Agua Negra*, Ahsahta Press, 1981; "What Was There To Do on the Plains" first appeared in *Desert Nights*, FishDrum Magazine; "Marilyn Monroe Indian" first appeared in *Going Home Away Indian*, Ahsahta Press, 1990; "Desert Nights" first appeared in *Desert Nights*, Fish Drum Press.

MIRIAM SAGAN

All poems are reprinted from *Art of Love: New and Selected Poems*, La Alameda Press, Albuquerque, New Mexico, 1994.

REBECCA SEIFERLE

All poems are reprinted from *The Ripped-Out Seam*. Rebecca Seiferle, The Sheep Meadow Press, Riverdale-on-Hudson, New York. Copyright © 1993 by Rebecca Seiferle. Reprinted by permission of The Sheep Meadow Press.

JOSEPH SOMOZA

"Precious" was first published by *Sell-Outs Literary Magazine*, January 1994.

ARTHUR SZE

"The Flower Path" and "Original Memory" first appeared in *Manoa*, vol. 4, no. 2, Fall 1992. "Whiteout" first appeared in *Dissident Song*, 29/30, June 1992. "From the Rooftop" first appeared in *Contact II*, vol. 11, no. 65/66/67, August 1993. Reprinted by permission of the author.

ANNE VALLEY- FOX

"Green Tara" was first published in *FishDrum*, vol. 1. "Waking" was first published in *Sending the Body Out*, Zephyr Press, Somerville, Massachusetts, 1986.

KEITH WILSON

"Sipapu: The Core" and "Portrait" were first published in *Retablos*, San Marcos Press, Cerrillos, New Mexico, 1980. "River Girl" was first published in *Bluefish*. "The Encircled Grove" was first published in *Longhouse*.

ROGER ZELAZNY

Quoted excerpts in the biography are reprinted from *For a Breath I Tarry*, New World Science Fiction, 1966. "Walking, of Course" will appear as the coda to the novel *Wilderness* by Gerald Hausman and Roger Zelazny, Tor Books, New York, New York, 1994.